AS IT WAS IN THE DAYS OF
NOAH

JEFF KINLEY

HARVEST HOUSE PUBLISHERS
EUGENE, OREGON

Cover by Dugan Design Group, Bloomington, Minnesota

Back cover photo © Tyler Rosenthal Photography

Cover photo © Alina Isakovich / Fotolia

Published in association with William K. Jensen Literary Agency, 119 Bampton Court, Eugene, Oregon 97404.

AS IT WAS IN THE DAYS OF NOAH

Copyright © 2014 by Jeff Kinley
Published by Harvest House Publishers
Eugene, Oregon 97402
www.harvesthousepublishers.com

Library of Congress Cataloging-in-Publication Data
Kinley, Jeff.
    As it was in the days of Noah / Jeff Kinley.
        pages cm
    ISBN 978-0-7369-6138-7 (pbk.)
    ISBN 987-0-7369-6139-4 (eBook)

1. End of the world—Biblical teaching. 2. Bible—Prophecies—End of the world. 3. Deluge—Biblical teaching. 4. Noah (Biblical figure) I. Title.
BS649.E63K56 2014
220.1'5—dc23

                                                                            2013050130

Printed in the United States of America

                14 15 16 17 18 19 20 21 22 / BP-JH / 10 9 8 7 6 5 4

To my four "listeners" who, like Noah,
acted on God's promptings.
Your faith inspires me.

Acknowledgments

Authors are always searching to find their next book project. However, in this case, the book found the author. This project began with a "crazy idea" that quickly morphed into a big step of faith. I owe a huge thanks to my agent, Bill Jensen, who initially saw the vision for the book and suggested that I write it. I'm grateful to my wife, Beverly, who fervently prayed with me about taking on this project. I also could not possibly have written this book without the aid of my "scribe," Stuart Kinley, who tirelessly typed in my original revisions and edits, and who also served as a second set of eyes. Finally, I'm indebted to the entire Harvest House team, who saw *As It Was in the Days of Noah* as a timely book for this generation.

Contents

Introduction

Perhaps no ancient story in human history captivates our attention as much as Noah and the Great Flood. The tale of the Ark is as old as time itself, with some 270 versions of it having been passed down through the ages by cultures around the world. From Assyria-Babylonia to ancient Egypt, China, and even Hawaii, each flood account bears striking similarities to the biblical narrative. Particularly amazing is that the majority of them describe a wicked population, a lone righteous man, and a universal destruction by water and an ark.[1]

Skeptics point to these "flood myths" as proof that the Bible has no exclusive right to this often-told prehistoric allegory. They claim Moses (or "whoever actually wrote Genesis") probably borrowed the common myth, adapting it to fit his Jewish culture and concept of God. They allege that the story of a man building a giant cargo ship to protect his family from a wrathful deity who will destroy mankind is nothing more than a fossilized fable. A fairy tale. Of course, the alternative explanation is troublesome—that the biblical account is 100 percent accurate down to the most minute detail, and that the Creator embedded the story in virtually every ancient culture as a testimony to its veracity. But God went a step further, taking care to document the event in a book for us.

Jesus Christ believed in Noah. And the Flood. And the Ark. In fact, nowhere in Scripture is there even the slightest hint that the man Noah, his story, or the worldwide Flood event is a metaphor, mythological tale, morality parable, or fictional tale. On the contrary, the reality of the Flood event is firmly established.[2] But of course you would expect this from the Bible, right? Even more amazing, however, is that Jesus links the historicity of Noah and his Ark to the certainty of coming prophetic events and His physical return to this planet.[3]

Further, Jesus prefaced His statements about Noah by claiming His words are so true they will outlast heaven and earth.[4] Or to put it another way, "Everything I say will come true," He asserted, "and you can bank on this truth."

To dismiss or deny the reality of Noah and the Great Flood, you need only to refute the person of Jesus Christ and His claims to deity, something no mortal has successfully accomplished in the past 2000 years. The historical reliability of Scripture (and thus the Flood event) is inseparably linked to the character and identity of God Himself. And while it's possible to have an accurate historical record without God's help, you can't have prophecy or the supernatural without Him. Undoubtedly, Noah's is the quintessential story of prophecy, divine intervention, and judgment.

With chilling accuracy, the Bible recounts this epic event that took billions to a watery grave.[5] What we find in Scripture is way beyond a Hollywood blockbuster. No computer-generated imagery, 3-D, or special effects here. And no fantasy flick slamming your senses with larger-than-life images and sounds depicting the horror of a global aquatic apocalypse.

Instead, it's something much worse.

As It Was in the Days of Noah will transport you back to a world you will hardly recognize. The sights and sounds of pre-Flood earth may disturb you. This story will adjust your perspective on humanity and even challenge your perception of God Himself. But it's also my hope you'll use the Flood narrative as a lens through which to view today's world, allowing you a glimpse through God's viewfinder. For it's through studying this past event that we can more clearly understand the present and more effectively prepare for the future.

As you read along, I encourage you to search the Scriptures for yourself. This Noah guy is way more than some ancient character in a book, and his R-rated story is definitely not for children. The following pages contain the uncut version, a chapter in humankind's history so unsettling that you may secretly wonder if it really happened the way the Bible describes. This book unveils the heart of man and the holiness of God. Therefore, we set sail in reverence. With that said, the seas may get a bit rough, so if you're ready, then climb aboard, grab a life jacket, and hold on.

You're about to discover how an old Sunday school story leaps forward in time, shedding light on today's generation and linking itself to yet another coming global judgment. But as you dive into Noah's story, you'll also find a reservoir of hope.

And a God who waits at an open door.

Jeff Kinley
Little Rock, Arkansas

1

The Days of Noah

I am sorry that I have made them.

GENESIS 6:7

A flood is coming. God is going to destroy this earth, including *you*, unless you repent.

This was the core of Noah's message. Simple. To the point. No beating around the bush. This preacher's sermon was plain, straightforward, and even uses an object lesson to illustrate the message's main point—the building of a very big boat. Noah's audiovisual sermon lasted 120 years.

And then the Flood came and destroyed them all.

Just like that.

But there's a bit more to this story. While describing the Flood drama, what is often lacking amid tales of the old man and the Ark, its animal kingdom occupants, and the terrible water judgment, is how *God* felt about the whole affair. We know in the end He brought judgment, but we fail to mention that the catastrophic event which annihilated mankind initially flowed not from a furious fist, but from a broken heart. God's Spirit was grieved. He actually experienced sorrow, an unusual concept to contemplate, particularly in the context of judgment. But there are facets of God's relationship with humankind that emotionally affect Him, bringing lament and regret to His Spirit.[1] That's because God isn't some stoic, emotionless, distant deity, but rather a Father who feels. He's not a crotchety old man with furrowed brow, yelling at the neighborhood kids for making too much noise. He's not sitting somewhere in the cosmos watching us and looking for some way to punish us for every wrong we commit.

To the contrary, His is a heart more tender than mortal words can describe. More affectionate than human thoughts can imagine. Remarkably, He is simultaneously compassionate and holy, gracious and righteous, merciful and just, forgiving and wrathful. And no contradiction or inconsistency exists between these attributes. His infinite qualities harmoniously complement one another in a manner and on a level far above our human understanding. This is the mystery of deity. He is God—transcendent, yet personal. Invisible, yet intimate. Everlasting, yet ever present with us. The God who floods also forgives. Regularly upstaged by animals and an Ark, the main character in this ancient drama turns out to be Yahweh Himself. He is the principal player and director, as the story begins and ends with Him. His presence is the backdrop to every scene.

In the Flood narrative, the action pauses as if in slow motion or freeze-frame. The story seems to stand still, and in these parenthetical moments we catch a glimpse of who God really is. We get to peer into His heart, seeing His character with refreshing, high-definition clarity. As with many epic episodes portrayed in Scripture, God provides us with a multi-angled perspective focused on a single incident. Through these verbal vantage points recorded for us, we see what He sees. In the story of Noah, we are granted access to those camera angles. Through this field of vision, we encounter among other things, a grieving God, heart torn in two over His creation's descent into decadence and moral madness.[2] We see how sin brings sorrow to Him, and in this case, how that sorrow set into motion a prophecy of judgment. In an ironic twist, we discover the only way God could save humanity was to destroy it and begin again.

This is how it happened.

After successfully leading a few million of his fellow Jews out of Egyptian slavery, Moses (a former shepherd turned deliverer) snaps a 400-year losing streak for God's people. The next 40 or so years Moses spends wandering around with them in an uninhabited no-man's land, better known as the Sinai Desert.

Sitting in his tent, Israel's deliverer takes a reed pen and papyrus sheet and begins to write the story of God and man—the *official* account. He describes the wonder of creation, the heavens, the earth, the stars, even the concept of light itself. He chronicles the creation of the seas, vegetation, creatures of the water, land and skies, concluding with His most creative work—making a human being in His own image and breathing the breath of life into his nostrils. This would be His greatest accomplishment. His magnum opus. His masterpiece.[3]

But it wasn't long before history's first humans, endowed with choice by their Creator, used their freedom to pursue self-gratification over God. This is the point in the story where the ink in Moses' pen takes on a decidedly darker tone. The celebrative chorus of creation now transitions to a regretful refrain as it traces mankind's downward spiral into sin and ruin. The Maker of Life would have preferred a different story line, one where Adam and Eve choose obedience over believing a lie. But it was not to be. And as ongoing evidence of this, all Moses has to do is lift his tent flap and observe millions who had made the same choice in the desert—abandoning faith in a good God to follow their own desires and designs.

And so, perhaps with heavy heart, Moses describes in detail the condition of planet earth more than 4000 years ago. Thanks to him, Genesis 6 is our backstage pass to the past—a private, behind-the-scenes tour of an age some deny existed while others try hard to forget. It's a chapter in human history even some Christians find hard to believe. But it's there, like a permanent stain on our record. Humanity's "rap sheet," chronicling our past crimes, offenses, and failures. An embarrassing episode in our family story. It's the relative that we prefer not to talk about. The ex-con uncle. The no-class cousin. The kinsman you don't "claim." The black sheep of the family. But there's no escaping it. And as our human family continued expanding, each successive generation grew worse and worse. Before long, we reached the point of no return.

Sex, Demons, and Depravity

Back in the Garden of Eden, God commanded Adam and Eve to "be fruitful and multiply, and fill the earth."[4] This was one mandate they and their offspring would have no problem obeying. Sex was good, and procreation plentiful. In our world of perversion and pornography, we may forget that it was *God* who thought up the idea of sex. We're pressured to think the sexual experience is some primal urge birthed through evolutionary development or a timed chemical release from the brain. Hormones and nothing more. Or worse, that it's some evil, satanic idea. But that's not true. Sex is a beautiful gift straight from the heart of God. He created it. It's *His* invention. He gets the credit. He also designed our bodies, minds, and emotions to actually *enjoy* the experience, even becoming exhilarated by it. He made sexuality desirable, a natural and very good thing.[5]

After previously acknowledging this, Moses then summarizes approximately 1500 years of life on earth, writing that "men began to multiply on the face of the land, and daughters were born to them."[6] Considering the average male life span then was several hundred years, Adam and Eve's descendants had plenty of time to procreate. Apparently they were pretty good at it too, causing an explosive increase in earth's population as mankind grew at an exponential rate.

Since the aging process was much more gradual and people were living longer, there were a lot of babies being born. But is it also possible that, before the long-term effects of sin completely ravaged the human mind and body, sex was even more pleasurable than it is today? Did Adam and Eve's fall into sin rob us from a greater experience in physical intimacy? Whatever the case, a result of all this sexual activity was natural and prolific procreation with no thought to limiting the size of the family. So by the time Noah arrived on the scene, earth's pre-Flood population could have easily been between 7-10 billion people.[7] But it wasn't this population explosion that displeased God. After all, He had commanded His creation to get busy with the task.[8] Instead, something else was grieving the Creator's heart. Genesis 6:5 states, "Then the Lord saw that the wickedness of man was great on the earth, and that every intent of the thoughts of his heart was only evil continually."

Wait, did you read that correctly? Did Moses really mean to write that? Did he actually say that *every* thought of *every* person was *only evil*? *Continually*? As in all the time? Is that even possible? Apparently so, and here's why:

We typically compare ourselves to others when it comes to morality. Stand yourself up next to Hitler, a terrorist, or some sex offender, and all of a sudden you're a saint by comparison. But when matched up beside God's pristine holiness and standards, you and I come up very short.[9] In fact, throughout the Bible, God repeatedly declares the human heart is full of sin, even going so far as to say that it is "deceitful above all things," and "desperately wicked."[10] Wow, God—tell us what You really think! So it stands to reason that if the well (heart) is poisoned, what comes up in the bucket (our actions) will be also.

Theologians call this truth "total depravity." But this doesn't necessarily mean every person on the planet today acts as sinful or as evil as he or she *could* at all times. It's not like we all max out and reach our ultimate "sin potential" every day. Rather, it means the deadly sin virus extends to every corner and component of our being—body, mind, and soul. In other words, like the law of gravity, the law of sin holds us down, dictating and influencing certain things about us. It drags down our thoughts, emotions, and desires. This self-centered narcissism informs and impacts our decisions, relationships, families, communities, and ultimately our nation and world. Put several billion people on this sin-drug, and the side effects are devastating. Genesis 6:5 effectively asserts that we were a planet of hopeless addicts. Total depravity on parade. Long before God's judgment came upon these people, they were already busy filling the earth with their sin and evil. They actually *were* as bad as they could be—all the time.

What's more, Genesis 6 pinpoints a specific area of life that was influenced by this sin stimulant. Perhaps no other area of desire (outside of breathing and living) is so powerful and intoxicating as sex. And as we've seen, it is a good thing from God. However, sexual appetite is also a natural narcotic, and when laced with evil, it becomes a potent and deadly drug. In a pre-Flood world already gone mad overdosing on sinful cravings, it's easy to envision a global, sexual free-for-all. If the Bible is correct in stating that earth's entire population was thinking only about evil 24/7, certainly those evil thoughts would have included sexual promiscuity, adultery, and perversion, as well as rape, prostitution, homosexuality and lesbianism, and pedophilia. Does that sound extreme or far-fetched? Considering that most of these aberrations and perversions have been prevalent among us *since* Noah's day, it's not a stretch to imagine how prominent they would have been in a world without *any* moral compass or restraint. Perhaps even worse than our wildest imagination. There were no gentlemen in those days, only "Gentlemen's Clubs." No honorable men, only selfish beasts. The pre-Flood world sported a level of sexual debauchery that would make even a present-day pervert blush. Moses waits 12 more chapters in Genesis before specifically describing how God felt about a society that practiced blatantly open homosexuality.[11]

The plot of a recent movie portrayed a futuristic society where, for 12 hours once a year, any and all behavior, including crime, is allowed.[12] Think of what our present world would be like if there were zero restrictions whatsoever on sexuality. If you want it, you go for it. If you desire it, do it. No one can tell you no. What would life be like in such a world? What would sex and sexuality look like if mankind's worst and most vile imaginations were permitted, even *encouraged*?[13] Now imagine no moral conscience issues, no marital boundaries, and no age restrictions. You get the picture. Noah's earth was one giant orgy. Every night a bachelor party. Every morning a hangover. Billions of people, young and old, threw off the tattered rags of Eden's ideals, indulging themselves in every kind of sexual experience, experiment, and perversion.

Yes, they really were *that* bad.

If you believe Scripture, you eventually arrive at a mental scene stretching the boundaries of human civility and decency. "*Every* thought. *Only* evil. *Continually*."

But there's evidence of a second tier to this moral anarchy. It's an underbelly of sexual perversion inconceivable even to a sinful human mind. Moses records, "The sons of God saw that the daughters of men were beautiful; and they took wives for themselves, whomever they chose."[14]

There is conversation among theologians and Bible scholars as to exactly who these "sons of God" were. Some suggest the phrase refers to Seth's descendants, described as God-seeking men.[15] Seth was Adam's son, a direct ancestor of Noah, and also included in the genealogy of Jesus.[16] So some read Genesis 6:2 and simply see a lot of marriage going on among Seth's godly clan. But there's another interpretation as well. Immediately after this statement, God says,

> My Spirit shall not strive with man forever, because he also is flesh; nevertheless his days shall be one hundred and twenty years. The Nephilim were on the earth in those days, and also afterward, when the sons of God came in to the daughters of men, and they bore children to them. Those were the mighty men who were of old, men of renown.[17]

It doesn't make sense for God to withdraw His Spirit from mankind simply because godly men married beautiful women.[18] What, then, would motivate Him to remove His Spirit and start a 120-year count-down to judgment? The implication, aside from the rampant, global evil mentioned later in verse 5, is that this particular marital union somehow contributed to earth's unbridled moral decline, leading to God's eventual retribution.

So who are these "sons of God"? This title (Hebrew, *bene Elohim*) is used elsewhere to describe supernatural beings, or *angels*, leading many to conclude these "sons of God" were angelic beings, or more specifi-cally, demonic entities.[19] Therefore, Moses was saying that demons were having sex with mortal women. Now that's a bizarre, foreign thought any way you look at it. However, the New Testament appears to sup-port this view, indicating the punishment for this unnatural act was to cast these demons into "pits of darkness, reserved for judgment [in hell]."[20] Jude 6 also mentions demonic angels "who did not keep their own domain [spiritual world], but abandoned their proper abode, He has kept in eternal bonds under darkness for the judgment of the great day." A portion of the angels had been expelled from heaven because they had allied themselves with Lucifer in his rebellion.[21] Because of this, the demonic host are now beyond redemption.[22] And evil itself originates in their spirits.

Given their corrupt nature, there is no higher demonic delight than to pervert God's design for His beloved humanity. Through their deviant sexual unions, these demons attempted to mimic what God Himself had done—to create a being in their own image.[23] They would try and duplicate what His creation (humans and animals) could do—reproduce after their own kind. This was a second attempt to make themselves "like the Most High."[24]

Had Satan, the master sin-strategist, succeeded in corrupting the entire human race through demonic infusion, he could have theoretically prevented the coming of the Messiah through the "seed" of the human woman (Genesis 3:15).[25] That would have been an ingenious and shrewd plan indeed had it come to reality.

But of course we know demons are spirit beings and do not have physical bodies. Further, Jesus said that angels do not "marry."[26] However, according to Scripture, they are still capable of inhabiting, possessing, and taking the form of human bodies.[27] In fact, angels did assume human form and were able to walk, eat, and even have physical contact with mortal men.[28] And from the perspective of Sodom's male citizens, these angel-inhabited bodies were fully capable of sexual activity.[29] So it is very possible that these vile, God-hating, demonic creatures either assumed human form *or* fully possessed existing males in order to have (perhaps forced) sexual relations with women. Either way, it further illustrates the depth of human corruption and wickedness in Noah's day. Can you see the devolution of man?

Sex in marriage.

Sex outside of marriage.

Unrestrained sex.

Perverted sex.

Abusive sex.

Depraved sex.

Demonic sex.

It doesn't get any more wicked than that.

What must the spiritual environment in Noah's day have been like if demons were having sex with women? Or what level of depravity existed if men were dominated by demonic spirits in this way? And, assuming it wasn't forced upon them, what kind of women would welcome or desire such unions?

Moses follows this up by mentioning that the Nephilim lived on the earth. This word is used only one other place in the Bible, referring to a race of giants who lived in the Promised Land.[30] The mere reported sighting of these Nephilim created such fear throughout Israel's camp that it discouraged them from entering their promised home. Instead, they consigned themselves to wandering like desert nomads for 40 years.

Were the Nephilim (root word meaning "to fall") of Genesis 6 an antediluvian race of giants resulting from a union between demons (or demon-inhabited men) and mortal women? Or were they unrelated to the demonic union, simply "mighty men," cruel tyrants who overpowered and dominated others? Whatever the case, it all still points to the existence of rampant, pandemic immorality filling the earth. There was virtually no place where sin had not penetrated and perverted mankind.

Are you starting to see it?

Planet Terror

But Moses isn't done just yet, as he records for us yet another degrading and damnable characteristic of humanity during the days of Noah: "Now the earth was corrupt in the sight of God, and the earth was filled with violence...*all* flesh had corrupted their way upon the earth."[31]

Billions of people, having long since jettisoned the Creator from their consciences, became violent in their dealings with one another. There is no discernible rule of law or order of government. And into this void of leadership and societal structure pours an angry spirit of chaotic violence. All over the world, man solves his problems and disputes by forceful aggression. Hostility. Fighting. Brutality and cruelty. Bloodshed rules. Savagery is the standard. God says the world was "filled" with this kind of violence, meaning it extended to every part of it. Every community. Every tribe. Anywhere there were people, there was violence and human terrorism. No home was safe, perhaps even from its own family members. It is not difficult to imagine widespread domestic violence in such a savage society. Given the fact that it would take thousands of years for the status of women to be elevated, imagine how men must have treated the opposite sex in this universal culture of chauvinism and sin. Verbal, emotional, and physical abuse. Violent domination of women. Violent beatings. Violent rape. Violent murder.

But the rising tide of sin didn't stop at the gender border. Women were not innocent parties in Noah's day, but were equally enslaved to evil in all its various female varieties.[32] They were just as complicit in wickedness, wantonness, and disregard for decency. There was no shortage of she-devils walking about God's relatively new world. Proverbs 29:16 states, "When the wicked increase, sin increases; but the righteous will see their downfall."[33] Simply put, the more sinners there are, the more sin there is. That was the case in Noah's day. People hurt each other. A lot. They fought. They wounded. They murdered. And it was violent. Every homicide was considered justifiable simply because of the mere *desire* to commit the act. "What's yours is mine, and I will kill you to get it," was their murderous mantra. People killed in revenge, for pure pleasure, curiosity, or even sport. Random killings. Senseless slayings. Spur-of-the-moment murders. Savage slaughters. Massacres of entire families or perhaps even whole people groups.

Sounds hard to believe, doesn't it? Like some primitive sci-fi apocalypse. How could we have been this *bad*? How could human beings lose all traces of dignity and decency and act like this? Wouldn't a common-sense survival instinct kick in at some point and bring relative order to such a world? Apparently it didn't. But why? The answer is found, in part, by understanding something about sin itself.

From Seed to Forest

It didn't take long in mankind's story for his jealousy and aggression to get the best of him, as the very first human born into this world became a cold-blooded murderer. Adam and Eve's firstborn, Cain, rose up against his baby brother and took his life from him. But how? And why? Did he strangle him in the field? Stab him with a sharpened stick? Crush his skull with a fist-sized rock?

Scripture doesn't reveal exactly *how* Cain committed earth's inaugural act of violence and murder, but we do have a clue as to his *motive*. The Bible tells us the two brothers each brought an offering to God—a sacrificial, ritual act of worship no doubt passed on to them by their parents. After Adam and Eve's sin excursion in the Garden, God provided animal skins for earth's first couple, covering the symbol of their sin and shame—their nakedness.[34] An animal (perhaps a lamb) was slain by God to make this possible. The point? A blood sacrifice is necessary to take away sin, an innocent life dying to symbolically cover sin and restore fellowship with God. And this ritual became God's prescribed pattern until the ultimate sacrifice was made on the cross.[35]

Abel was a "keeper of flocks," while Cain was a "tiller of the ground."[36] Two necessary occupations in a primitive agrarian world. So when the time came for offerings to be made to the Lord, each son brought what he had—Abel, a choice lamb, and Cain, a portion of his crop. But God accepted Abel's offering while rejecting Cain's. Scripture says Abel's lamb was "better" than Cain's crop, and that it was offered in *faith*.[37]

The nature of their offerings (animal vs. grain) wasn't as significant as the fact that one was offered in faith and the other more out of duty or self-effort. Abel's lamb was the "firstling," or best of the bunch, while Cain's grain was simply some of his crop.[38]

But it was Cain's *response* to God's rejection of his offering that planted the seeds of murder. He became "very angry," and his "countenance fell."[39] In other words, he was jealous, furious, and dejected. And right here is where God's grace reaches out to Cain. God knows where this is headed, so He gives Cain an "out." And some hope. The Lord tells him he has no real reason to be angry, but to simply change his heart (toward God) and his attitude (toward his offering). If Cain would, by faith, give God his best sacrifice, instead of keeping it for himself, he would experience happiness and not dejection.

"But," God obligingly warned him, "if you do not do well, sin is crouching at the door, and its desire is for you, but you must master it."[40]

Compacted within this one statement is a potent dose of practical theology. God tells Cain (and us) that sin is a "living" principle, a powerful force for evil, and that it lies in wait for him like a ferocious lion in tall grass. The Lord adds, "[Sin's] *desire* is for you." This Hebrew word *teshuqah* (tesh-oo-kaw) signifies a very strong desire to dominate.[41] In the context of this conversation, God spells it out for Cain.

"You can't let sin rule you, Cain. On the contrary, *you* must master *it*."

History's first son is now at a critical fork in the road with a very important choice to make. He can let his anger and disappointment fester and spread within him, or he can take charge of his emotions and master the sin that is waiting to devour him.[42] Yet sadly, even God Himself couldn't talk Cain out of his sin, so deep had his self-addiction become. Meeting his younger brother in the field (maybe even crouching in secret like sin had done to him), he satisfied his anger by brutally murdering his brother.

And violence was born.

Behind the scenes, the covert co-conspirator in this first-ever murder was Satan himself. The apostle John later wrote that Cain was "*of* the evil one."[43] Satan, Jesus said, "was a murderer *from the beginning.*"[44] He is the silent partner in violence, the invisible instigator to brutality and bloodshed.

And so anger, jealousy, and murder were birthed at the very dawn of civilization, soon becoming prevalent throughout the whole earth and eventually prevailing over all humankind. It may sometimes appear that envy, jealousy, or anger are relatively harmless emotions. Normal. Expected. Tolerated. Even enjoyed. But when allowed to take root in our hearts, the results are usually disastrous. Jesus later compared anger to murder itself.[45] Sparking in humanity from its beginning, this violent spirit soon spread like a West Texas brush fire, ultimately engulfing the entire planet.

The violence of Noah's day illustrates the frightening *power* of sin itself. Imagine going to your doctor, and following a routine X-ray, you're told there's a baseball-sized mass growing in your abdomen. That would probably get your attention, right? That's because you have proof in a physical X-ray, something you can see with your own eyes. You also have a trained medical professional informing you about your condition. You'd be a fool for simply ignoring his words, dismissing the X-ray as a forgery or fabrication created by some doctor to scare you. In reality, you'd most likely take *him* at his word, and take your *condition* very seriously. The problem with sin, though, is that we don't think it's *that* bad. The things God calls sin we often ignore, wink at, or even keep as playful pets.

Today we lack a healthy respect for the danger, power, and influence of sin—both that found in the world and that which resides within our own sin nature. Like a deceived drug addict, we think we can keep it "under control." After all, we're not murderers or perpetrators of violent crime, right? So all things considered (and *especially* in comparison to Noah's world), as a human race we're doing pretty well. Or so it would seem. But what we fail to realize is that God has placed some restraints in the world that are currently holding back sin's floodwaters. These moral levees weren't present in Noah's day. More about that later.

In a pre-Flood humanity, sin became a lethal virus, a plague spreading from parent to child and person to person. It was "heirborn" in their DNA. And it was manifest through sexual perversion, wickedness, hatred, aggression, and violent behavior. And Noah's contemporaries were eaten up with it. It consumed them—man and woman, boy and girl. No one was immune. It respected no geographical boundaries. It was equally in women as it was in men. It flowed like a river through every town and village like their only source of water. They drank it during the day and binge-drank it in the evenings.

Theirs was not a pleasant world in which to live. Evil was king. People hated one another, and the whole planet hated its Creator. It was Mardi Gras on steroids. Every day was a riotous, rebellious rejection of the One who made them. Insanity and lawlessness reigned. Human rights didn't exist—only human *wrongs*. In the absence of righteousness, sensuality, violence, and demonic activity filled the void. The image-bearers Yahweh made had transformed themselves into a global mass of moral chaos and wickedness. God's magnificent creation of man had become a story gone horribly wrong.

This, then, is the strength, scope, and potential reality of life without God.

The Last (Righteous) Man on Earth

Noah found favor in the eyes of the LORD.

GENESIS 6:8

In the midst of this worldwide sin-frenzy, God found one man who stood out among billions. "Noah found favor in the eyes of the LORD."[1] Described as a "righteous man, blameless *in his time*," Noah was a man who "walked with God" (Genesis 6:9). Though not perfect, Noah nevertheless had integrity. And while not without blemish, Noah was still blameless, or a man of high moral character and reputation. In contrast to his peers' perverse, hateful, and violent character, he remained pure, decent, and civil. There was no dirt on Noah. He felt the pressure to conform to his generation's ungodliness, but he also felt called to be distinct in character and lifestyle.[2]

The challenge of being in the world's culture involves not being consumed by the sin inherent in it. Unquestionably we who are Christians are meant to be *in* this world, but we do not derive our identity or values from it because we are not *of* it.[3] Using wisdom, we can stay connected with people and society without allowing ungodly attitudes, beliefs, and conduct to shape or influence us.[4] Christians are intrinsically no better than anyone else, and Jesus condemned those who accessorized their faith with an attitude of arrogance.[5] We're called to demonstrate humility, love, and compassion, even among those with whom we strongly disagree. This can be a difficult dance, and it often means being the lone, dissenting voice. Or the only righteous one. It typically means swimming crosscurrent and even upstream. Following God may even lead to decisions and behaviors that bring ridicule, mockery, and even hatred.

Noah knew the drill.

He was righteous "in his time." He followed God *in the now*, responding in the context of his own generation. Intent on walking with God, he had remained unstained in a filthy world—not through self-righteousness, but rather self-preservation. He was righteous. But exactly how did Noah get to be so righteous in God's eyes? What was his story? How did Noah become "Noah"?

Legends of the Fall

Noah was 480 years old and already righteous prior to his Ark-building days, so he obviously had some previous history of faith. And as we trace back Noah's family lineage, we make an interesting discovery. What we uncover is a long, strong heritage of godly ancestors. For Noah, this heritage came through his father, Lamech. Scripture records an unusual statement Lamech made upon his son's birth. Concerning his newborn, he remarked, "This one shall give us rest from our work and from the toil of our hands arising from the ground which the LORD has cursed."[6]

This statement gives us insight into who this man was. Not only does it sharply contrast with another man with the same name, but it also tells us he was a prophet who foresaw great things for his son.[7] Lamech's prophecy lamented sin's curse and looked for God to bring relief from it through his son, Noah.

Also significant is the fact Lamech acknowledged Yahweh as God. This direct reference to God tells us Noah had a dad who *believed*. Considering the spiritual climate of his day, Noah no doubt received his first exposure to faith through his father. Many years later, the Lord instructed Israel to pass on faith through the context of family.[8] Noah's God-fearing father lived a "perfect" 777 years, and then died.

Tracing back further, Lamech's dad would become a legend in his own right, but for very different reasons. Methuselah holds the distinction of being the longest-living human in history, according to the biblical record. He lived 969 years, just a few years shy of a millennium.[9] However, there's something even more fascinating about Methuselah that we'll discover in the next chapter. This amazing ancestry continues with Methuselah's father, Enoch. Like Noah, he also "walked with God," and apparently he was pretty good at it too. Unlike every other man in Moses' list of genealogies, Enoch "walked with God; and he was not, for God took him."[10]

So close was this man to God that Scripture says he actually skipped death! The writer of Hebrews backs up Moses' claim.[11] What kind of man must Enoch have been for this to happen? And exactly how did he please God so much that it qualified him for such a rapture? According to Hebrews 11, it had a lot to do with exercising *faith*.

Keep in mind that Enoch lived in the same wild, wicked world as his grandson Noah. Sustaining faith in a hostile, ungodly environment is not an easy way to live. But Enoch was more than just a good example to his generation. He also opened his mouth and spoke out for his God. Scripture describes Enoch as a man who prophesied about the second coming of Jesus Christ.[12] Can you picture the courageous faith of this man? He was the first prophet mentioned in the Bible, foretelling judgment that would take place at the end of time. But considering the moral context and climate of his day, Enoch's prophecy was a double-edged sword, cutting to the hearts of his own generation. With confidence and boldness, he defended God's honor in a wicked world.[13] Enoch's words paint a dark portrait of judgment upon "all the *ungodly*" who have committed "*ungodly* deeds which they have done in an *ungodly* way." These ungodly sinners also spew verbal hatred toward God. This portrayal of the last days' generation matches Moses' words in Genesis 6:5 concerning the unceasing wickedness of Noah's day.

The rapture of this man up to heaven is one of the Bible's greatest mysteries, and Enoch's "death-free fraternity" has only one other member.[14] Considering the scathing nature of his prophecy, it's possible God snatched him away to save him from a cruel death at the very hands of the ungodly people he prophesied against.

Continuing with Noah's lineage, we land on a man named Enosh, the son of Seth and grandson of Adam. It's during this period of time that men began to call on the name of the Lord.[15] Lost through Cain's rebellion and absent because of Abel's death, Adam and Eve's faith makes a strong comeback through son Seth and grandson Enosh.

What emerges in this family tree is nevertheless clearly a very strong presence of godly men. A seemingly unbroken chain of faith was faithfully passed down through each successive generation, with the baton of belief landing in Noah's hand, whereupon he gripped it firmly. His ancestors had modeled a strong relationship with the Lord, and this is a major reason why Noah "walked with God." What a legacy to inherit! Faith has a way of diminishing from generation to generation. Not so in Noah's case. Like a priceless heirloom, faith was a family treasure handed down from generation to generation.

Though obviously not faultless, Noah's ancestors were nevertheless faithful men during difficult times, following God in their own generations.[16] Imparting truth and spirituality through the context of family and real-life examples is especially meaningful in a world hostile toward God.

Practically speaking, that's how Noah got to be Noah. His faith came from those who came before him. And it is to this righteous man that God speaks the most unusual words ever uttered to a human in earth's short history.

The Voice

Envisioning biblical events is difficult for us to do at times because they happened in another time, culture, and language. They also occurred during a unique era when God related to His people in a markedly different way than He does today. No one lately has seen a river divide, witnessed the dead raised, or watched while someone walked on water. You probably can't recall ever seeing the sun stand still or 5000 people eat dinner from a few loaves of bread and a couple of scrawny fish. You've probably never heard the actual voice of God either. That's because, though He definitely still performs miracles today, there are no longer biblical prophets and apostles performing supernatural signs authenticating His message. Paul made it clear that during the church age, the simple, supernatural truth of "Christ and Him crucified" would be God's main miracle message.[17] Rest assured, signs and miracles will make a strong comeback in the final days of planet earth, when supernatural wonders will again become a common occurrence.

But God does supernaturally speak directly to Noah, and Moses records the incident like it was an ordinary thing, which of course it was for him, being he was *Moses*.[18,19] As we mentally transport ourselves back into this pre-Flood world, it's fascinating to consider the communication between God and man, both in its nature and frequency. What must it have been like to actually hear God's voice? For the human ear to receive words straight from the Creator? And this voice was unmistakably recognizable, in that Noah never once questioned whose voice he was hearing.

Since Noah was already a righteous man who walked with God, this probably wasn't the first time he'd heard God's voice. He and the Lord had history together. So the strange thing here is not that God spoke, but rather the *content* of His words. Throughout the Bible, God occasionally asks His children to do unconventional things. Sometimes His commands seem inexplicable, even bizarre.[20] A cursory glance at these examples makes God seem arbitrary, odd, and a bit avant-garde in His dealings with man. However, upon closer examination of these stories in their context, there emerges a discernible purpose behind each of them. God never does anything without divine design and objective, though admittedly His plans are not always immediately visible or understandable. Everything He proposes comes from a mind of infinite intelligence, and our inability to comprehend them only highlights the limited scope and understanding of our finite minds. Isaiah makes reference to this reality:

"My thoughts are not your thoughts, nor are your ways My ways," declares the LORD. "For *as* the heavens are higher than the earth, so are My ways higher than your ways and My thoughts than your thoughts" (55:8-9).

God is saying, "I don't think like you do. And you don't think like I do." That's because our brain holds about a communion cup's amount of knowledge while His capacity for wisdom and understanding is more like the universe—*big*! That's an immeasurable contrast in capacity. And yet we still think we have better ideas about life and how to live it than He does.

Go figure.

So God speaks to Noah. And with His first-ever bizarre command explains how He is going to destroy mankind because of their corruption and wickedness. He then charges Noah with the task of doing something that had never been done before, something so weird and out of the ordinary that Noah was sure to become the laughingstock of his generation. Yahweh gives this righteous man detailed blueprints for constructing what seemed like a monument to madness. Specifically, these plans call for the construction of a gigantic structure that would save Noah and his family from coming judgment. His blueprint reveals the massive ship to be 450 feet long, 75 feet wide, and 45 feet high. To put it into perspective, that's some 100 feet longer than a football field, including the end zones. This mammoth rectangular box is equal to the capacity of 522 standard railroad boxcars, able to hold 125,000 sheep-sized animals. Three stories tall, with each floor measuring 15 feet high, it was to be constructed of "gopher wood."[21] Once cut, hewn, and planed, the wood would then be sealed with pitch, a glue-like substance made from resin.[22] This would have made the Ark virtually waterproof.

The reason for this random, seemingly ridiculous request is because God is going to "destroy [all flesh] with [including] the earth."[23]

After giving Noah the Ark's measurements, God repeats the reason for His odd command: "Behold, I, even I am bringing the flood of water upon the earth, to destroy all flesh in which is the breath of life, from under heaven; everything that is on the earth shall perish."[24]

God's global water judgment will kill everything that breathes. He also promises to make a special covenant with Noah and his descendants after the Flood has passed. But for now, there's work to be done. A lot of work. After Noah constructs this bigger-than-life object, he is to take "two of every kind [of animal] into the ark...male and female."[25] The next verse adds that God Himself would bring the animals to the Ark. Perhaps exhibiting a first-ever migratory instinct, tens of thousands of animals will follow God's invitation to safety and survival.[26]

Once they arrive at the giant vessel, they will all enter through a lone door in the side, no doubt reached via a long ramp. If God can speak through a donkey and direct a whale, and Jesus can control fish, then certainly these creatures would have no problem responding to their Creator.[27] Sadly, animals can often be smarter than humans in that way.[28]

Now all Noah has to do is build a ginormous floating zoo.

Rain Man

What God asked this righteous man to do was crazy enough, but it was compounded by one important detail: It had never rained on earth before. Ever.[29] Instead, Scripture says, there existed a vast body of water in the sky hanging like a tent canopy above the earth.[30] This canopy effectively filtered out the sun's harmful ultraviolet rays, also accounting for man's extended life span before the Flood. Before sin entered the picture, death was not a part of humanity's design. Had we not sinned, we would never have died.[31] We were meant to live with God forever.

Corresponding to the sky canopy of water, God also created a mist that regularly rose from the ground below, watering vegetation, plants, and crops.[32] These two sources would later account for the great reservoir of water used in the flood.

So even though it had never even rained a drop on the earth, God tells Noah to build a boat, which at that time would have become the largest object ever made with human hands. As far as we know, no one had ever conceived of such a thing as a boat. It was a foreign idea, and it would have seemed preposterous and unnecessary. Like building a rocket ship in Jesus' day. Considering the *nature* of this task, the *context* in which it was given, and the amount of *time* it would realistically take to accomplish it, Noah's acceptance of this mission proved one thing beyond a shadow of a doubt.

The man had faith.

And this one fact would make him as odd and eccentric as the Ark-barn itself.

Noah's undertaking would not be a weekend DIY project, or something he worked on in his spare time, or after work in the evenings.

Keep in mind there were no lumberjacks. No chain saws. No power tools. No logging trucks. No sawmills. No boatyards. No Home Depot! And no cranes or construction crews. This massive job would all be done with muscle and a whole lot of elbow grease. Oh, and there was also no crew of hundreds laboring around the clock to build this massive lifeboat. Just Noah and his three boys, though at this point they wouldn't be born for another 20 years![33]

So what did Noah have to look forward to? What did his future look like? What did the Lord's quirky command mean for him? In short, this God-sized task would require arduous work and backbreaking labor. Chopping. Cutting. Hauling. Hewing. Sawing. Hoisting. Hammering. Planing. Painting with pitch. Repeat process. Again and again. For 120 years! That's 1440 months of blisters and backaches. Or roughly 43,200 days of long labor. The equivalent of finishing a project in 2014 that you began back in 1894, or beginning one in 2014 and working nonstop until 2134!

You can bet that during that 120 years, Noah's generation took notice. His construction project was without a doubt the talk of the region, and possibly the entire world as far as we know. You couldn't miss it. It surely became a landmark of sorts, as in, "You take a left at the 'Ark thing' and my house is down that road about a half mile." Whatever else Noah had planned for the second half of his life had been put on hold by God. His schedule was replaced by Another's agenda. This mission had come straight from the Top. God's plan for Noah's future and hope would involve a lot of hard work.

What Noah was asked to do was difficult and challenging, requiring him to be "all in." That's because genuine, risky faith is rarely comfortable or convenient. For Noah, there would be no time for vacations or sightseeing, as his deployment in God's mission would be a long-term one. He would surely be thought a fool for his obedience. Beyond question, his generation would eventually label him an idiot. A complete buffoon. They would say he was wasting his life. Living in a dream world. That he had a screw loose. Building a useless wooden box for an imaginary god.

And besides, what kind of God would lay such a burden on a good man like Noah? Why would God ruin Noah's life like this, turning him into a carpenter-slave? Furthermore, what God would be so cruel as to destroy His own creation? And what kind of arrogance must Noah possess to think he alone knew what was going to happen to the world? Who was he to predict the future? Who was he to condemn others, claiming *his* God was the only way of salvation? That seemed neither fair, nor reasonable, nor loving.

So people undoubtedly made fun of Noah, mocking both him *and* his God. But after several decades of ongoing construction, did they begin to ignore Noah and his labor of lumber, or was it simply too hard to resist a daily drive-by taunting? Did gangs and tribes hurl insults at him and his family? Or did they hurl more than insults? Did fathers bring their children to gawk at "Noah's Folly"? Was he considered to be like the chimpanzee exhibit at the local zoo—amusing but harmless? Was he an easy target for anyone needing a lighthearted laugh in their day?

But in spite of guaranteed unpopularity and ridicule, Noah persevered, taking his job from God seriously. He prepared the Ark "in reverence," in light of heaven's warning about the coming flood.[34] He believed in things that hadn't happened yet. However, he went beyond just preparing a boat. He also attempted to prepare his generation as well, even proclaiming the truth (about the Flood and judgment) to the people in his day.[35] For this, he was given the title "preacher of righteousness."[36]

Sawing. Lifting. Hammering. Hoisting. Persevering. Proclaiming. Preaching.

Believing.

This man was either certifiably off-the-charts crazy or *very* peculiar. Out in left field. There was surely no other explanation for his bizarre, unusual behavior. Except maybe One.

Weathered Faith

Noah was fully persuaded concerning the reality of something he couldn't yet see. And that's exactly what faith does. It enables those who believe to see the unseen. To know the "not yet." To charge ahead in confident obedience no matter how outlandish, ludicrous, or counter-cultural it makes them appear. And God honors those who choose His "ridiculous" ways over the conventional "wisdom" of man.[37]

One man or woman with faith can stand against an army of antagonists. And Noah's naysayers were legion. He was outnumbered billions to one.

But considering the physical, spiritual, and social implications of his herculean task, did Noah ever experience episodes of doubt? Did Lamech's son ever waver in his faith while working on his century-long project day in and day out? If King David, the apostle Peter, and John the Baptist had significant moments when their faith grew razor thin, it's reasonable to assume Noah also had them as well. Surely he lay in bed some nights during those 120 years, wide awake with throbbing back pain, gashed leg, or swollen and bruised knuckles, wondering, "God, is all this really worth it? Is this flood really going to happen or did I imagine it? Is my boat going to float, or will I sink and drown like the rest? Did You really speak to me all those years ago, or am I wasting my time and life? Are the skeptics and cynics right in what they say about me? Will I be proved a fool? Is this the only way You can save us? Isn't there any other *easier* way to accomplish Your will?"

While Noah may not have experienced chronic, continual doubt, he, like all believers, surely suffered self-doubt and satanic attacks. His own sinful nature likely kicked in as well, flooding his thoughts with occasional apprehension and periodic self-pity. He also got tired. Worn out from wielding an ax, working a saw, and swinging a hammer. And the thousands of regular insult-hurlers threatened to chip away at the faith-wall protecting his heart. Noah was, after all, still just a man. But in spite of his mortal limitations, he had learned over time to develop and exercise his faith-muscle. It was this strong belief that got him out of bed in the morning. Flexing his faith got him through the soreness and pain. It insulated him from the verbal barbed arrows of those who ridiculed him.

Believing in God for something great sounds noble enough. It's even considered admirable. Attempting something big for Him is a good thing. But the reality of life in a sinful world is that *real* faith is often bloody and dirty, difficult and challenging. It's the kind of faith that goes beyond theory to *doing*. It travels from your head and heart to your hands, feet, and mouth. It's not the kind of faith you talk or write about. It's the kind you *live*.[38] It's not hypothetical, but practical. Though invisible, others can see it. It's a faith that *works*. It sacrifices and suffers if necessary. It's *bloodstained* faith. The kind marked by bruises and scars. A bit frayed on the ends. Tattered and torn in places. Worn *thin*, but not worn *out*. Looking beaten, but still bold. It appears defeated, and yet it remains determined. And best of all, it's *yours*. Like a favorite pair of shoes, the more it's used, the more comfortable it feels.

This is battle-hardened faith.

It's not pretty, but it sure is beautiful.

Our romantic ideals about being strong believers are brought into perspective as our faith-race hits the 20- or 30-mile mark. How strong would your faith be if everyone in your world was against you? If every person with a heartbeat thought you were a fool? What if they wanted to take your life because of your faith? Or sabotaged your efforts to accomplish your mission for God? Did Noah suffer at the hands of saboteurs? Did he suffer setbacks because someone set fire to lumber or stole tools and materials from him? In any case, he kept on doing what God had asked him to do, even down to the smallest detail.[39] That's what faith does. It obeys. And there's nothing glamorous about it. Just glorious.

Noah had faith.

Ours is a generation of quick fixes, no waits, and instant communication. We impatiently tap our fingers, waiting for a 30-second microwave dish. We swipe our debit cards because writing checks takes too long. We auto draft ourselves into expediency. We expect immediate results. We want what we want, and we want it *now*! And many Christians have subconsciously embraced this mind-set. We expect immediate deliverance from our problems and grow spiritually weak when they linger on. We expect quick fixes to marital struggles, even if it took years for us to get into the perilous predicament we're in. We seek shortcuts to Bible knowledge, maturity, and expertise that took others decades to earn. Pastors want growth and maturity in their churches but fail to make the huge investment of time required to actually *make disciples*. In our personal growth too we expect spiritual muscles without spiritual exercise. We feel it's our right to succeed or to be given success, promoting ourselves from little league to the big leagues.

If we could get maturity and discipleship from a drive-through window, Christians would line up for miles. Then even that would take too long, and we'd demand it in a phone app. We get out of breath when asked to run the long distances of faith. We're often content to settle for the *appearance* of spiritual knowledge, maturity, and strength. We desire all the benefits but none of the struggles. We want the perks without the pain. Progress without perseverance. Success without suffering. We want to look good spiritually and have great faith, but we don't want to saw and sweat, hammer and hurt. Not for long, anyway. We just want a big boat and a story to tell about how it was a "God thing." We're weak and out of shape. And that's why it doesn't take much suffering to bury the average Christian under a pile of defeat and depression. We're spiritually lazy, proven by the fact that most believers go for years or even decades without sharing their faith. I wonder how much real persecution it would take to crush the Western church? What would it take to cause us to fold under the pressure?

Honestly, we just want to build a pre-fab, awesome-looking Ark to impress our friends and post on Facebook, and to do it all without blisters and inconvenience. But that's not Christianity. And that kind of faith is nowhere found in the Bible. When we visit God's Hall of Fame, we encounter heroes with real, raw faith.[40] There we find suffering, sacrifice, obedience, and men and women living like strangers in a strange land. We meet some whose promise from God wasn't fulfilled in their lifetime. Men who passed over pleasure to endure pain with God's people. Women who overcame a difficult past. Men who conquered kingdoms, did righteous deeds among unrighteous people, escaped execution, and instilled fear in their enemies. We discover those who held up under torture, mockery, beatings, and prison. Some were stoned by angry mobs, while others were sawn in half. They endured financial and physical hardship for the sake of the One who loved them.

And they did all this because of a faith that few in our day know anything about.

God says they were people of whom this world was not worthy.[41]

Christians talk big about God and faith, and we're good at it. We make promises to Him we don't keep. We speak the lingo well, fluent in "Christianese," convincing others that ours is a deep, strong, and heartfelt belief. But often we end up living an illusion, fooling most of the people most of the time, and sometimes even fooling ourselves. We become practical atheists, acknowledging God with our lips while our hearts remain content to please ourselves. Like He's not even there.

Noah didn't have that option.

The old carpenter's mission and circumstances demanded that he be in it for the long haul, with no room for casual commitment. After all, how do you "fake" an Ark? He either had to "go big or go home." God and everyone around him would eventually know if Noah's faith was the real thing. There were no shortcuts for this guy. No corners to cut. No alternate routes. It was all or nothing.

That's what living in the days of Noah does for your faith. It sifts it, filtering the fake right out. It forces you to declare with your mouth, and then to back it up with your life. There's no one for Noah to impress here. He knew his faith would be offensive to his peers and that his prophecy of coming judgment would not go over well with his generation. And as if to add insult to injury, he would build a colossal cruiser as a perpetual reminder to the world that God wasn't happy with them.

Noah wasn't about to make his generation's Who's Who.

We often casually declare that God will give us the grace we need when hard times come. We say that because it freaks us out to think about actually having to *develop* the faith-muscles needed to survive life's coming trials and storms. But strong faith (the kind that keeps you from imploding or self-destructing during the difficult and stressful seasons of life) isn't handed out by God like free cookies at a bake sale. Instead, it's matured, strengthened, and refined over much time and through thousands of small, daily choices to trust Him.

Noah's faith went beyond building an Ark. It was about the daily walk to the forest to fell another tree. Mixing pitch. Notching wood. It was all about the "dailies." Strong faith is forged through walking with God through the routine highs and lows of life. It's acquired by depending on Him in the seemingly insignificant issues we encounter each day. It's nurtured and grown through incremental risks taken for Him. Big faith almost always requires making tough choices. It involves recognizing that this world is not our home.[42] Faith "in the now" looks *beyond* the now. Genuine trust in God is a gut-check, demonstrating what you actually believe is real, true, and most valuable in life.

Noah had *strong* faith.

He grew accustomed to living by faith and continued walking with God over the course of 120 years of preaching and persevering. This long process solidified his faith. As a result, Yahweh became his motivation, power source, safety net, and reward. And over time, his hard work finally began to pay off as his big project took shape. No longer was his workplace merely tree trunks, stacks of lumber, and a huge pile of sawdust shavings. In time, the outline of a ship's bow slowly appeared, rising up from the grassy plain. And with every hammer blow, a call to repentance and faith echoed throughout the land. More than a century's worth of daily, audible warnings were given to a deviant people. And then, Lamech's lunatic son drove in the last peg.

It was time.

Noah's Ark was finished.

At God's command, the boatbuilder and his entire family ascended the long ramp and entered their ship of safety. Following them was a parade of paired animals brought to him by God.[43] For a full seven days before the rain fell, Noah and his family received animals, settled themselves inside the Ark, and prepared their passengers for the long journey ahead. The day of grace had now come to a close. God had patiently waited for 120 years. His message had been sent. There would be no excuses and no second chances.

After everything had been made and secured, God Himself supernaturally shut the door of the Ark, signifying the time for salvation had officially passed.[44] And yet even with the Ark door closed and sealed, earth's evil inhabitants still could not conceive of what was about to happen. Billions went about their business as usual. Their enslaving obsession to self and sin had so blinded them to truth that they simply continued life as always, unconcerned about Noah, his message, or the fact that they were all about to die.

And there was nothing anyone could do about it.

Deluge

The flood came and destroyed them all.

JESUS IN LUKE 17:27

For Noah and his family, those seven days in the Ark prior to the Flood were filled with work—loading and sorting some 50,000 animals into pens, distributing food, and cleaning up in what would soon become a full-time job for the duration of their aquatic adventure.[1] Anticipation filled their hearts as they prepared to sail into the first-ever "uncharted waters." But their journey into the unknown also brought a deep sense of relief and reverence. Despite repeatedly envisioning this day for 120 years, nothing could have fully prepared Noah and his shipmates for what they were about to experience. He must have pondered what this impending judgment would be like, dreaming about it in his sleep, and his daytime thoughts often filled with images of water, wind, and waves. But he could never have fully visualized the reality of the coming destruction of planet earth. Would the boat to which he had devoted so many years actually float and withstand the test of the raging floodwaters? Would it survive the crushing wave of the Almighty's wrath?

He was about to find out.

Pausing to rest his calloused hands, Noah contemplated their perilous voyage. There was nothing left to do inside but light another lamp and wait.[2]

The time had passed for preaching one last sermon in the hope that someone, anyone, would respond to his message of repentance and salvation. Given a choice, we might vote for Noah's generation to get one more chance. After all, that seems fair...*just in case* they change their minds about God. That's what a good and loving God does, right? He has to extend the day of grace all the way up until the very last second.

Or does He?

Though God is more gracious, compassionate, and merciful than the human mind can fathom, Scripture also tells us His patience has a limit.[3] Those who treat lightly His patience and kindness, stubbornly refusing to repent, store up wrath for themselves.[4] When the free offer of grace is rejected, nothing remains except judgment. Repentance is always urgent. God's justice always severe.

And to most, this is a very inconvenient truth.

God understands well the nature of the human heart.[5] It's not natural for us to choose God because sin has enslaved our minds, emotions, and desires. Our minds are steeped in thinking that opposes God, focusing instead on pleasing self. We have an emotional aversion to God and His "restrictive" ways. The people of Noah's day resented God and were even hostile toward Him.[6] Their sin-filled hearts made them allergic to the Almighty. They didn't feel like obeying Him. And there wasn't the slightest desire to submit to Him. If they wouldn't turn to God after 120 years of incessant invitations, there would be no sudden change of heart now that Noah had completed his insane construction project.

Instead of giving mankind one *last* chance, God had given them one very *long* chance. One hundred and twenty years of opportunities. More than 43,000 sunrises and sunsets to consider Noah's offer of salvation. In their minds, there were no more signs of impending judgment on the day Noah entered the Ark than when he felled that first tree those many years ago. Everything on the earth continued along as it always had. There were no more ominous clouds than before. No rumblings in the sky. No thunder and lightning. No warning bells. No sirens. No panic in the streets. No more reason to believe Noah the Nutcase now than there was yesterday or 100 years ago. Nothing had changed. Life just went on as it always had. There was no compelling motivation for Noah's generation to abruptly break character and fall on their knees in repentance.

And God knew this.

Finally, after ascending the long ramp, the last animal crosses the Ark's threshold. Noah stands in the vessel's doorway, a symbol of salvation for those who enter through it.[7] Now with all safely inside the Ark, Noah takes one last look at his home, workshop, and world whose terrain was about to be forever altered. Earth would never be the same after this. His was the last look at life before the Great Flood. All those years spent building the Ark by faith. Now he had entered into it by faith. And as the ramp door is supernaturally lifted by the Giver and Taker of life, perhaps out of the corner of his eye Noah catches sight of a young female villager walking in the distance. He turns his gaze toward hers and their eyes briefly meet, whereupon the woman smiles, wagging her head at the crazy, quirky old man who had become the derision of the known world. The butt of every joke. A fool's fool. A teller of tales. The inventor of fables. A prophet of doom like his ancestor, Enoch.

The huge door shuts with a deafening thud. The seven days are up. It's D-Day. Zero Hour.

And one of the saddest moments in human history.

Liquid Hell

Scripture portrays an unfiltered story of the Flood, and one more violent and disturbing than we're accustomed to. Moses wrote, "In the six hundredth year of Noah's life, in the second month, on the seventeenth day of the month, on the same day all the fountains of the great deep burst open, and the floodgates of the sky were opened. The rain fell upon the earth for forty days and forty nights."[8]

Moses made certain that successive generations and civilizations would know the exact day and manner in which the Flood came. Surely no future generation would be so ignorant or arrogant as to suggest that this global deluge had never happened, right? So to be on the safe side, Moses recorded for the ages the precise *day* it occurred, forever documenting an accurate account of when the Lord destroyed the earth.[9]

And the deluge came—suddenly, unexpectedly, and furiously, bringing damnation to the world. The day of Yahweh's wrath had arrived. And the earth trembled as angels watched in wonder and holy fear.[10]

Scripture faithfully recounts precisely how the Flood occurred. First, the "fountains of the great deep burst open." Supernaturally induced seismic shifts opened up subterranean storehouses of water located beneath the earth's surface. These massive reservoirs burst open, spewing unimaginable quantities of water up into the atmosphere through large ground openings.[11] Geysers of water exploded through these earth-vents, both on dry land as well as under the oceans. This caused an immediate, rapid rise in sea level, flooding low-lying areas and perhaps fueling earthquake-driven tsunamis that likely killed millions. As these underwater geysers erupted, the ocean's depths increased, creating water deposits that remain today.[12]

Following these subterranean fountains, the "floodgates of the sky were opened."[13] Working in tandem with the fountains of the great deep, the release of water stored in this global vapor canopy accounts for a worldwide flood. A veritable water world was formed as earth's surface simply disappeared underwater—along with houses, farms, buildings, businesses, livestock, and forests. Mountains too. Nothing escaped the mighty torrents of water.

This event caught earth's pagan population completely by surprise. Despite repeated warnings, the mere suggestion of such a catastrophic event was considered preposterous. The only people who believed in it were religious fanatics. Reality and truth for these nonbelievers was determined by majority or popular opinion. Being fully intoxicated with themselves, there was no room for a Creator. And only the "crazy ones" believed in Noah's absurd tale of judgment.

When they had reached working age, Noah's sons became an indispensable part of his construction crew. But perhaps there were other family members who pitched in as well? Noah's father, Lamech, lived 115 years after the construction work began, so he may have lent a hand.

And then there was Methuselah.

Say My Name

We met Methuselah earlier, but there's more to his story—and his direct connection to the Flood. Methuselah was 849 years old when God spoke to his grandson about building the Ark.[14] It's uncertain how virile he was at that age, but we do know he had already lived about 88 percent of his eventual life span.[15] So it's unclear whether he was helping out—fetching tools, hauling lumber, making measurements, swinging a hammer, or applying pitch, or if he simply sat quietly on a nearby stump, sporting a long, white beard, cane in hand, watching his grandson toil away. But hammer or not, Methuselah played a key role in the flood narrative.

God, as the Master Storyteller, wrote a subtle twist into the biblical script. And through the luxury of hindsight we can more fully appreciate and understand it. Even though Methuselah lived longer than anyone, it's not the length of his life that's so remarkable.[16] Rather it's something about his name itself that catches our attention. "Methuselah" means "when he is gone, it shall be sent" or "his death shall bring it." But bring *what*? What will be *sent* when Methuselah is gone? Examining the birth records in Genesis, we discover that the Flood occurred when Noah was 600 years old. That's not a big deal until we realize it's also the *exact year* Methuselah died. This is not some secret, hidden Bible code. It's simple math.[17]

His death shall bring it.

God sent a warning to earth not through a highway billboard or a church sign, but instead embedded within a man's *name*. Arguably among the oldest of billions living in his day, Methuselah's notoriety nonetheless came from his name. A prophet like his father, Enoch, Methuselah could predict the future without even uttering a word.[18]

As long as Methuselah was alive, there would be no flood. As long as he was breathing, judgment would be delayed. Every time his name was mentioned, the prophecy injected into his name was announced to his culture. Each time *Methuselah* was heard, God broadcast a message of grace to the human race. Noah understood the meaning of this name, perhaps even referring to it in his preaching. Having his granddad around gave Noah increased confidence God would let him finish the Ark in time. Even so, I imagine some in his immediate family grew a little nervous anytime Methuselah got sick, especially near the end.

A walking and breathing Methuselah meant there was still hope and grace. Nine hundred and sixty-nine years' worth of open doors to salvation. That's much more than the 120 required to build the Ark. It's the equivalent of nearly 350,000 days. Well over a quarter of a million chances for faith and hope. Grace extended beyond belief. Judgment delayed beyond necessity. And yet not a single soul responded. To those who won't believe a message about judgment, a message of grace is of little significance. If you don't believe you have a disease, then the offer of a cure has zero importance.

We aren't told exactly how or when Methuselah passed from this world to the next. Did Noah lower his granddad's millennium-aged body into the ground only to promptly hear God's voice commanding him into the Ark? Or was he murdered by some God-hating gang that was fed up with hearing *that* name associated with *their* judgment? If so, did such an act drain the last drop of patience from the heart of God? Was Methuselah's death what triggered the final seven days leading up to the great deluge? Or was God even more precise than that? Could those first floodwaters have coincided with Methuselah's last breath as he watched his grandson wave a solemn goodbye from the Ark's doorway?

All we know for sure is that in the very year Methuselah died, the Flood came. Exactly as the 969-year-old prophecy said it would. Coincidence?

I don't think so.

The Flood judgment arrived as a world tsunami, and the carnage was more horrifying than any human disaster before or since. Thousands of underground dams bursting forth were met by celestial torrents of rain unleashing massive water blankets down onto the earth. This continued nonstop for 40 days and 40 nights. The devastation was brutal. The panic, widespread. The death toll, indescribable. Can you envision the terror gripping the souls of those who had mocked the seemingly senile boat maker? Swallowed by monster waves, they cursed Noah and his God as they frantically scrambled up the hills for safety. Did mobs race en masse toward the Ark, banging on the door, demanding to be let in? Did others dog-paddle their way to the massive wooden ship, pleading, begging, clawing while their lungs filled with water? Or was there simply no time for them to do so because of the catastrophic nature of this event?

The scope and magnitude of this divine disaster invoked angry fear from every calloused heart. Today when a natural disaster occurs, some religious personality claims the calamity is a direct judgment of God due to widespread moral decline. We dismiss such persons as publicity seekers, religious fanatics, nutcases, or hate mongers. And rightly so.

But this was different. *Very* different.

This time we *know*. God said so.

For the billions who drowned outside the Ark and around the earth, this was no natural disaster brought on by weather formations, ecological imbalances, or climate change. No, this was wrath-of-God stuff, and they knew it. For the very first (and last) time, earth's population grasped the gravity of their depravity and the magnitude of their offense against the holy Creator. And though they had received exactly what they deserved, no discerning believer ever gloats over such a judgment. Instead, we shudder in reverence as we mourn the loss of those unrepentant souls.[19]

And the waters kept rising. Rapid was their upsurge, eventually raising the massive cargo ship, lifting it from its dry dock and causing it to float.[20] Its mammoth door was securely shut, locked like a bank vault, with only One holding the combination. And that's how every living thing that remained on the earth was killed.

Sound like a children's story to you?

What Kind of God Would Do This?

Some see the Flood account as some sort of divine temper tantrum, as though God has a short fuse or anger-management issues. It all sounds so harsh and cruel. So over the top. Extreme overkill. What kind of God would do such a thing to His own creation? And how do we reconcile the common perception of this *wrathful* Old Testament deity with the *meek* and *gentle* Jesus of the New Testament? Was the total destruction of mankind really necessary? Was it justified? How do we understand this act in light of Christ's directive to "love your enemies"[21]? Does God make one set of rules for us and another for Himself? Could this simply be an example of a scary religious fable meant to frighten people into obeying the rules?

From a superficial flyover of the facts, it would appear so. But as with any deep and difficult truth, we have to get our feet on the ground and dig a little in order to discover the real story behind the story. And doing so requires a certain degree of openness and honesty. So let's grab a shovel and dig in.

Obviously, either the Flood really happened as the Bible describes or it didn't. If you conclude it isn't historically plausible or suited to your theological taste buds, then you're free to go your merry way and carry on with your life. If, however, you want to understand why a loving God could destroy those made in His image and how the God you worship can be both gracious *and* vengeful—if you seek to know why love didn't win over wrath—read on.

The Flood indisputably drowns out all other episodes of divine retribution recorded in Scripture—beating out the Ten Plagues, Sodom and Gomorrah, and that time God made the earth open up and swallow people.[22] Jesus Christ confirms and validates that the events of Noah's day "happened," that "the flood came" and "destroyed them all."[23] If you believe Jesus was God in human flesh, then there aren't a whole lot of options available. Believing in Him links you to the truth about the Flood. Otherwise, you're left with a Jesus who was a liar, deceiver, or simply didn't know what He was talking about.[24] In any of those scenarios, He could not be the sinless Savior, but rather merely a Jewish rabbi, fallen and flawed like the rest of us. Nice and loving perhaps, but certainly not God. Just a misguided, wannabe Messiah. But since He believed in the account of the Flood, He also understood there was no contradiction between God's actions then and His own teaching in the first century.

So given that Jesus is onboard with the Ark thing, how *do* we understand God and His actions here? How do we make sense of the worldwide slaughter of all peoples regardless of social status, age, or gender? Young and old. Women and children alike. Even the animals! Birds and bugs too. Everything that breathed. They all died. How do we embrace this without feeling like God is some sadistic monster?

A.W. Tozer wrote, "What comes into our minds when we think of God is the most important thing about us." [25] Scripture's authors understood this, and wrote to tell us *who God is*. To begin with, the Bible describes Yahweh as the *only* God.

"I am the Lord, and there is no other; besides Me there is no God." [26]

Take note, "God" is spelled with a capital *G*, signifying He has no equals and no peers. [27] That one thought pushes the boundaries of postmodern political and religious correctness, flying in the face of an age that embraces all religions and faiths as equally valid. Unfortunately for other faiths, this Triune God (Father, Son, Spirit) claims exclusivity to deity, making every other world religion, spiritual pursuit, and philosophical system either invalid, a creation of man's imagination, or at worst, demonic in origin. Effectively dismantle the deity of Jesus, and nothing else about Scripture or Christianity makes sense. And this same God claims to have created the universe, earth, and mankind out of His divine power. [28] This elementary truth about our Creator-God is encoded both in nature as well as in humanity itself—abundantly displayed in the heavens and indelibly chiseled within the heart of man. [29] So He stands alone as the only God and Creator.

God is also *sovereign*, meaning He is in control of the universe and all things. [30] He rules over all, superintending humanity without violating man's ability to choose. *Sovereignty* means He is King, and that there is no earthly ruler, president, prime minister, despot, or dictator who remotely compares to Him. [31] It is before *this* monarch that every knee will bow and every soul will be weighed. [32]

So if that's really true, how worthy must this King be to deserve the sincere praise of untold billions? Just who *is* this God?

Scripture portrays Him as One who defines majestic royalty and sovereignty. Like Job, this deep realization prompts us to acknowledge that God is way out of our league. And we simply put our hand over our mouth, shut up, and bow in awe of Him.[33] How amazing is this God? He is so sovereign, wise, and powerful that He can take even the worst of man's sin and turn it into great good for us.[34]

But Scripture also portrays God as holy, righteous, and just—words used a lot in church, but rarely explained. His holy nature means He is completely different from us and the model of moral perfection. And this holy character dictates and directs His actions. That's why all of God's ways are, by definition, "righteous."[35] His holiness and righteousness are inseparable. God's holiness refers to His character (who He is), and His righteousness refers to His conduct (acting in harmony with His character). *Justice*, then, is God administering the consequences to those who keep or disobey His righteous standards. And because we lack God's knowledge and wisdom, His justice can seem out of sync with our timetable or liking. Sometimes this justice appears too light, delayed, or even nonexistent, while at other times it comes across as way too harsh and heavy (like the Flood).

This same God is also both wrathful and gracious. These are not, however, contradictory concepts, but rather harmonize perfectly in light of His character and good pleasure. The Flood is a primary example of God's wrath, pouring out His displeasure on a perverse planet. Simultaneously, we see His abundant grace in saving and preserving a remnant of humanity. God would have been equally just had He wiped out all of mankind and started over with a new "Adam and Eve." Or He could have chosen to simply punt the idea of humanity altogether. And had He done this, you and I wouldn't be here. What kind of God would do this? A sovereign, holy, righteous, just, wrathful, and gracious God. The disturbing truth about Noah and the Great Flood finds its roots in God Himself.

What Kind of People Would Deserve This?

Understanding the nature of God is only one side of the coin. In reality, there's a cause-and-effect relationship between our understanding of God and a true perception of *ourselves*. How we view God directly impacts how we see ourselves. As we appreciate the One, we can clearly see the other. We live in a culture that shuns words like *evil* and *sinful*, especially when they're applied to people. It makes us uncomfortable. Terms like *good* and *evil* are defined not by some unchanging standard from God, but rather by how things make us *feel*. It is precisely this kind of thinking that leads many to see the idea of a worldwide Flood as a mean, heartless, hateful, and disgusting act by a cruel and unloving God. Why? Because we can't imagine an entire planet's population being worthy of such a fate. Therefore, the mere suggestion that those who perished in the Flood actually *deserved* this death (and much worse) is brushed off as cold and even sadistic.

However, this is exactly the kind of objection Scripture anticipates, describing the human race the following way:

> So this I say, and affirm together with the Lord, that you walk no longer just as the Gentiles also walk, in the *futility of their mind*, being *darkened in their understanding, excluded from the life of God* because of the *ignorance* that is in them, because of the *hardness of their heart*; and they, having become *callous*, have given themselves over to sensuality for the practice of every kind of impurity with greediness. But *you* did not learn Christ in this way.[36]

In other words, without God, our thoughts are fruitless, vain, and futile. We are unable to see or understand the truth. There is no real life in us.[37] We are ignorant of His ways. Our hearts are hard and calloused from repeated refusals to submit to Him. Sounds a whole lot like Noah's generation, doesn't it? So is it any wonder the reality of God and His actions are so repulsive to those without Christ and biblical understanding? Because of sin, we are blind to reality and therefore invent our own. We say things like, "God would never..." And that's why we struggle with accepting truth, especially when it's troubling or distasteful.

We're also naturally resistant to God's inherent right to do as He pleases. Whenever God does or allows things we don't agree with, we become inwardly hostile, rejecting Him in favor of our own supposedly better ideas about how the world should work. As sinners, we demand freedom of choice, and yet deny that same right to a perfect and infinitely wise God. Even as believers, we still sometimes don't like Him being the Boss, particularly when it's uncomfortable or inconvenient. When life confuses or frustrates us, we secretly question His motives and decision-making skills. We do this because we have a deep-rooted issue with thinking we're smarter than He is. Casually confessing "He's God and I'm not" goes deeper than just saying it. It means embracing the truth that we're part of a fallen race. Finite. Messed up. Shortsighted. Selfish. Sinful.

And deserving of wrath. Every one of us.[38]

Even so, the Flood wasn't in God's original script for mankind. His first draft called for His creation to respond to Him in love, intimacy, relationship, and obedience. Our God didn't wring His hands in delight at the destruction of those who rejected Him.[39] On the contrary, His Flood judgment was a mixed drink of sorrow, wrath, and grace—terribly tragic and yet miraculously consistent with His divine character. However, His tolerance for man's rebellion had come to an end. And so God "blotted out every living thing."[40]

It was now time to start over.

A New Beginning

Following 40 days of nonstop rain and many more days of prevailing water, God makes good on His promise to Noah, and the floodwaters slowly begin receding.[41] The Ark comes to rest on an Ararat mountain, specific location currently unknown.[42] Seventy-four days later, the mountaintops become visible, and a new system of hydrology begins returning water on the ground to the earth's atmosphere via evaporation. Finally, when the land is dry enough, Noah exits the Ark and finds a very different world from the one he had left behind a year earlier.[43] The amount of habitable land had shrunk as the oceans increased in size. Mankind would now experience the changing of the seasons (Genesis 8:22), including storms, severe weather, blistering cold and blazing heat, earthquakes, and other natural disasters.

But none of that mattered at the time. Noah was eager to get off his oversized houseboat, and his first act upon disembarking was to build an altar to God. Using the clean animals he had taken with him, he offers a sacrifice of worship and thanksgiving, presumably a ritual his family had practiced for generations.[44] This pleased the Lord very much, prompting Him to declare:

> I will never again curse the ground on account of man, for the intent of man's heart is evil from his youth; and I will never again destroy every living thing, as I have done (Genesis 8:21).

Fulfilling His previous pledge, God promises never to wipe out all mankind like this again.[45] Following this declaration, He establishes several additional precedents concerning the future of humanity, the most well-known being the creation of the rainbow sign.[46]

Noah now trades his hammer and saw for a plow and potter's wheel. After planting a vineyard, in due time he partook of its fermented fruit and became drunk—no, make that he got *wasted*. The winemaker ended up in his tent naked and passed out in a drunken stupor.

Noah's youngest son, Ham, walked in on his inebriated dad. The Bible says he "*saw* the nakedness of his father,"[47] then told his brothers about it. For this act Noah would curse the lineage of Ham's son, Canaan, prophesying subjugation and slavery for them.[48] But what could Ham have possibly done to his dad that would motivate Noah to curse his own grandchildren? The Bible isn't specific, but there are two main possibilities, and neither of them are very good.[49]

Whatever the actual nature of Ham's actions against his father, it was serious enough for Noah to basically condemn a whole branch of Ham's family tree. His penalty for dishonoring Noah would be to have a son who would dishonor *him*. The Bible records that the Canaanites would later be put into subjection by General Joshua and afterward by King Solomon.[50] Because the Canaanites are extinct, obviously no such curse exists today.

Noah's act and his son's response illustrate how extensively the veins of sin run in us. But the incident also clearly demonstrates that righteous people, no matter how devoted or sincere their past obedience, are never immune from temptation and the pleasurable lure of sin. One of the most refreshing features of the Bible is that it never shies away from recording the sins of its saints. Instead, it lays them out in graphic detail.

The Flood demonstrates that God, though patient, will not tolerate sin forever. He has set a limit on what He will endure. And though devastating and deadly, His is nevertheless a just and righteous judgment. Noah's earth was corrupted beyond belief and redemption. And God's wrath on the inhabitants was deserved. The Flood helps us understand how evil and lost mankind can be. It teaches hard lessons about the ongoing fallibility of the human heart and our own struggle with sin. It tells us that even after a global judgment from God, mankind did not magically get better. That serves as compelling evidence as to why we still desperately need a Savior.

4

Carpenter Prophet

As it was in the days of Noah, so it will be
at the coming of the Son of Man.

JESUS IN MATTHEW 24:37 (NIV)

Fast-forwarding some 2000 years, the One of whom Enoch spoke now walks the earth. It's a Tuesday, spring of AD 30.[1] The location is a popular hillside just outside Jerusalem. Jesus the Christ has gathered a handful of His closest disciples for a private meeting, very much in contrast to the swelling crowds He regularly engaged. It's the last week of His earthly life, so He's spending it away from the limelight to be with His inner circle of followers. He knows that come Thursday evening, it's all going down—everything for which He has striven these past three years. All the teaching, traveling, and time spent with His disciples. Every word He spoke, and every step He took, even His very purpose for being born, will climax Friday morning in a bloody mist of whips, fists, and nails.

Unlike His disciple friends, Jesus was well aware of what awaited Him at the cross. He knew excruciating agony and torture would come crashing down on Him like a tidal wave of torment, and that God would have to treat Him as sin itself.[2] In just a few short days He would fulfill His role as the Lamb of God, our willing Substitute.[3] He had never known anything but unbroken communion with His Father. But Friday morning, all that would change as God abandoned His Son and blasted Him with the full fury of hell itself.

However, that time would come soon enough. For now, He was looking forward to some quality time with the men in whom He had invested the truth these last three years. Therefore, these final few days were particularly special to Him. And so, reclining on that Olivet mountainside, He imparts to them a wealth of instruction to pass on to future disciples.[4]

Curious, they ask, "Tell us, when will these things happen, and what will be the sign of Your coming, and of the end of the age?" (Matthew 24:3).

Jesus had just finished informing them that their beloved Jewish temple, currently still under construction, was going to be utterly destroyed.[5] Even after all He had taught them, they still expected their Master's earthly kingdom and reign to come immediately.[6] Therefore, Jesus' temple prophecy didn't quite fit their end-times template—hence their question. But instead of addressing the *when* (timing) of His coming, Jesus instead focuses on the signs *leading up* to His eventual return. The disciples could not conceive of their Lord leaving them, nor could they yet comprehend the concept of the church age. And so addressing their question, He leaps forward to a time the Twelve would personally never see and could never have possibly imagined.

Jesus explains that a series of signs will appear in the days prior to His return. These signs will resemble "birth pangs."[7] Labor pains occur toward the very end of a pregnancy, beginning sporadically and then increasing in frequency and intensity, leading up to the actual birth of a child. Jesus says these birth pangs will occur during a seven-year period known as the *Tribulation*.[8] Scripture describes this awful chapter in earth's history as a time when God will once again bring worldwide judgment on mankind. But unlike the Flood, it won't be a single event, but rather a *series* of happenings that occur (some simultaneously) over a span of seven years all across the world. While Jesus doesn't cover every prophecy or detail, He does give the disciples an informative overview of things to come. And as He describes this apocalypse, no doubt the disciples' eyes widened in wonder while their bearded jaws dropped.

Matthew 24 unveils for us some of the signs that will precede Jesus' second coming:

Sign #1—False Christs (verses 4-5)

In uncertain times, opportunists are quick to capitalize on people's fears and insecurities (remember the Y2K scare?). Immediately prior to this time of Tribulation, Scripture says Jesus will snatch up His bride (the church), rescuing her away from the "wrath to come." Millions of people will suddenly, without warning, vanish from the planet. Christians know this event as the *rapture*.[9] This moment is a catalyst that inaugurates the seven years of the Tribulation. It will leave our world in great emotional, economic, and spiritual turmoil. Into this dark void will pour a glut of self-proclaimed gods and gurus, all making their own claims to truth, knowledge, and prophecy.

Jesus later says some of these gods and gurus will be demonically empowered, able to show "great signs and wonders, so as to mislead, if possible, even the elect."[10] Our world currently boasts no shortage of false faiths, philosophies, misguided messiahs, spiritual gurus, mystic sages, and charlatan counselors. The apostle John warned that "antichrist is coming, even now many antichrists have appeared; from this we know that it is the *last hour*."[11] As we approach the final days, expect to see an increase of false prophets and counterfeit Christs, even in a culture of skeptics and atheists. Until then, John admonishes, "test the spirits" to see if they confess Jesus as the Christ.[12]

Sign #2—Wars and Rumors of Wars (verses 6-8)

The end of the age will be marked by intense international military conflict. Some of this may result from a post-rapture global economic collapse in which powerful countries absorb weaker ones by force. Considering our world's current economic and geopolitical climate, this is not at all hard to imagine in our lifetime. Major countries are currently defaulting on their financial obligations, sinking into virtual bankruptcy, and becoming dependent on foreign aid for economic survival. Even the United States is flirting with financial collapse on account of its astronomical debt and its potential to default on its obligations.

But this economic situation pales in comparison to the potential for increased warfare in our world. A single act of terrorism, suicide bombing, or missile launched by a rogue regime or maniacal leader could, overnight, catapult us into a world at war. Some of these future wars may even be racially or religiously motivated. But despite the cause, no country is safe from the threat of military conflict. The anxiety and uncertainty Americans felt on 9/11 will be multiplied many times over on an international scale during this time of trouble. Even now, unstable relations between nations have made peace a fragile commodity that could easily be shattered by the slightest provocation.

Sign #3—Famines and Earthquakes (verse 7)

It's estimated that some 1,300,000 earthquakes occur each year in the world, with over 1600 of them measuring a magnitude of 5.0 or above on the Richter scale.[13] The 2010 earthquake in Haiti alone killed more than 150,000 people. Truly, the very earth itself is unstable and unpredictable. Jesus prophesies end-times earthquakes in "various places," and Revelation 6:12 mentions a "great earthquake" so powerful it causes a mass chain reaction of volcanic eruptions.[14] The ensuing ash and debris will cloud the atmosphere, producing a worldwide "blackout." This combination of multiple wars and earthquakes will wipe out world food supplies, creating global hunger.[15] Millions of people will be displaced without food sources or drinkable water. The faces of starving children so commonly associated with third-world countries will be seen in developed nations.

The disciples' heartbeats collectively rise as Jesus continues. "But," He warns, "this is just the beginning. It's going to get much worse."[16]

Sign #4—The Persecution of Believers (verse 9)

When asked whether people will become Christians during the Tribulation, I confidently answer, "Yes!" Though God's judgment will be falling on the world's inhabitants, He won't be finished saving people yet. It's unsure exactly how the rapture will affect those left behind, but it's safe to say this global event will definitely get people's attention. Many may finally be convinced that those "Jesus freaks" were right all along. In desperation, they will cry out to God for salvation, and He will turn none of them away.[17] But faith in Christ will come at a great price in the last days. Panning His disciples' spellbound faces, Jesus announces, "Then they will *deliver* you to tribulation, and will *kill* you, and you will be *hated by all nations* because of My name."

During the Tribulation, there will be an international pandemic hatred of Christians, with "all nations" joining the party. Because of the rapture and the subsequent economic chaos and conflict, those who become believers during the Tribulation may be turned into scapegoats for the world's ills.[18] In reality, this animosity is merely a tangible demonstration of the world's seething anger toward Jesus Christ. You would think the disturbing events of the last days would drive people to their knees, but instead, many of them will vehemently curse God.[19]

Exactly as they did in Noah's day.

It's estimated that some 100,000 Christians are murdered for their faith each year.[20] That amounts to hundreds daily, and doesn't include believers killed in places without communication to the outside world. There are many martyrs who die in obscurity and anonymity, their fate known only to God. But as with the first martyr, Stephen, Jesus Himself stands to honor and greet them upon their homecoming. We don't know how many will be martyred in the last days.[21] We are told, however, the chosen means of end times execution: beheading.[22]

Even now the seeds of hatred toward Christians have taken root. Speak out against immorality, and you're hated. Stand up for traditional marriage, and you're branded a bigot or a repressive bully. Claim Jesus is the only way to God, and you're a narrow-minded fanatic. So it's not difficult to imagine this current simmering animosity toward Christians reaching a boiling point following the rapture. Until that day, things will grow increasingly worse, with Christians becoming more marginalized in society, our views and values growing increasingly unpopular, even despised. Though we are to pursue peace with all people, our faith may still unintentionally incite hatred in some. Jesus says, "Count on it."[23] We should never return hate for hate, but neither should we lose our loyalty to our Savior.

Sign #5—Apostasy and Betrayal (verses 10-13)

Persecution always sifts true believers from those with a mere professed faith. In this future period of intense Christian persecution, "many" counterfeit Christians will turn away from the faith. In the early days of the Tribulation, many seemingly repent, trusting in Christ.

But when persecution and the threat of death arrive at their doorstep, their facade of faith will fall away, leaving behind a heart bent on self-preservation. Even today, the slightest opposition to faith often causes those who profess to be believers to abandon their allegiance to Christ and His church. This is to be expected, for as Jesus earlier illustrated to His followers, decisions don't make disciples, devotion does.[24] One way we know our faith is real is by seeing our affection transfer from self to Jesus. These future faux believers will demonstrate their true colors, giving up their Christian friends and even family members and allowing them to be arrested and murdered.[25] In a satanically inspired persecution, those instigating this slaughter will utilize persuasive methods, motivating people to turn Christians in. Failure to comply may result in monetary fines, loss of government benefits, or even death.

Jesus' words sound so unreal. It's hard to imagine something so backward and barbaric happening in a civilized society like ours. But historically speaking, every generation tends to minimalize past world tragedies and human atrocities, at times even trivializing them. The further in the rearview mirror these events are, the smaller in significance they become. Like faded photographs or black-and-white movie reels, their importance belongs to another time and generation, not our own. So we forget things like the Jewish Holocaust and red-letter dates like December 7, 1941, because they no longer affect us. How long do you think we have before 9/11 disappears off our memory radar?

Similarly, it's hard to envision a future worldwide persecution of Christians. When Christian persecution comes to mind, the average believer typically thinks of that which occurred under the Roman Empire. However, there have been many believers martyred under government-sanctioned persecutions throughout history. But none of this persecution will compare to the massive torture and slaughter of Christians in the Tribulation's early months.

What makes Jesus' prediction even more difficult to believe is that we fail to realize how much the world *already* dislikes Christians and their God. It's the prevailing spirit of the age, like gathering storm clouds. This hostility will reach a fever pitch in those days. Combine the collective sin nature of the world's inhabitants with a global hatred of believers, and a new genocide will be born.

There will be blood.

Contributing to this, Jesus adds, will be many false prophets who arise, misleading the multitudes, possibly including those who formerly professed faith in Christ.[26] The teachers of this new era will persuade multitudes away from what they allege is the barbaric, bloody religion of a crucified Messiah. Demonically inspired, they will give people what they really want—a sense of escape, meaning, hope, and purpose during difficult times. Some of these religions will involve the actual worship of demons, various kinds of idols, and drug-induced magical arts.[27] Sounds preposterous, right? And yet up until recently, there was a pagan bookstore just blocks from my own home selling idols and magical arts resources on how to contact and worship demonic spirits. More evidence Satan is still alive and well on planet earth. Finally, as a result of vanishing biblical morals and values, wickedness and lawlessness will increase (Matthew 24:12). Even love itself will be a scarce commodity. Just like the days of Noah.

Sign #6—The Gospel Preached to the Entire World (verse 14)

In the midst of planet-wide pandemonium, God will once again demonstrate His grace and offer the gospel, thus giving humanity an "out." Believers have long wondered how it's possible to ever saturate the entire world with the gospel. The church has trained, commissioned, and sent out thousands of gospel ambassadors all around the world, with more missionary resources available now than ever before. We have faster travel, the Internet, advanced communications, and even cutting-edge Bible translation software. And yet the harvest remains plentiful, with almost three billion people on the planet (41.2% of the world's population) still having never heard the name of Christ![28] So how will God accomplish this herculean feat within such a short time span, especially considering He's already taken all His mouthpieces to heaven (Christians), and those who remain and believe are being slaughtered like cattle?

According to Revelation, God will use three means to broadcast the gospel during the first half of the Tribulation. First, He will send two men, anointed and authenticated by God, as His prophet-preachers. Designating them as "my two witnesses," He will endow them with supernatural powers, including the ability to shoot fire from their mouths at anyone who tries to harm them or thwart their mission! They will also possess the power to prevent rain, turn the waters into blood, and smite the earth with plagues at will.[29]

They will travel around in rough camel hair coats, and their message in those desperate days will be one of repentance and salvation. Then, at the end of their 1260-day ministry (3½ years), God will allow the Antichrist to kill them.[30] The Antichrist will place their dead bodies in the streets of Jerusalem for 3½ days while the entire world celebrates their deaths, even exchanging gifts to commemorate the occasion![31] It will be an international holiday. An unholy Christmas. So hardened and evil will our stubborn planet be that it actually rejoices in the assassination of those who proclaim the gospel of Jesus!

But God always has the last word. After 3½ days, He will breathe life into the witnesses' dead bodies, and they will stand on their feet, terrifying those partying around their temporary graves. The two witnesses will then ascend to heaven in plain sight of all, an event no doubt broadcast globally on television and immediately shared with millions online. This will fuel worldwide wonder at the event. Adding an exclamation point, the Lord will cause an earthquake in Jerusalem and 7000 people will be killed, with those escaping death giving glory to God![32] This is likely a partial fulfillment of Paul's prophecy concerning Jewish salvation.[33]

Some believe one of the two witnesses is Enoch. Having never tasted death, he who prophesied the first global judgment in Noah's day is said to return to do the same for the earth's final judgment. However, because of their supernatural powers and similarities, I believe these two witnesses to be Moses and Elijah.[34]

The second way God will proclaim the gospel worldwide during this time is through 144,000 Jewish evangelists. These young men will be chosen, protected, and commissioned by God—12,000 from each of the 12 tribes of Israel.[35] They will have the name of God Himself written on their foreheads as further testimony of their purpose.[36] These men will also be sexually pure, truthful, blameless in lifestyle, and fiercely loyal to the Lamb, Jesus Christ.[37] Our generation desperately needs this same commitment and loyalty today; we need to be men and women of integrity who live to honor the Lamb! Referred to as "first fruits," this Jewish army of gospel proclaimers may comprise the first responders to the ministry of the two witnesses. They will live for one purpose—to herald the good news of repentance and salvation through the Messiah.[38] What would happen today if even a small fraction of professing Christians viewed their lives and treasures as a means to spread the gospel with such fervency?

Third, in this age of renewed signs and miracles, God will blanket the earth with a final proclamation of the gospel message. He won't limit Himself to using a human voice; instead, He will send an angel from heaven to broadcast the announcement.[39] This special angel, whose identity is currently unknown, will proclaim the good news with a "loud voice" that is heard all around the planet![40] God, who is able, will make sure every human ear hears this invitation to salvation in his own language—as it is delivered to *every* nation, *every* tribe, *every* tongue, and *every* people. Never again will anyone ask, "What about those who have never heard of Jesus?"[41] No individual will be able to stand on the day of judgment and claim, "But I never knew about You, Lord!"

And this angel's message? "Fear God, and give Him glory, because the hour of His judgment has come; worship Him who made the heaven and the earth and sea and springs of waters."[42]

The angel's sermon will be short and to the point: Turn from trusting in yourself and bow before the Creator-God. Fear the One whose judgment is falling on your world. Worship Him! The angel identifies this God as the One who made the heavens and earth. Peter prophesied that in the last days, people will deny God as Creator.[43] The Bible repeatedly claims it was God who made the world, the universe, and humankind, ruling out other theories of origins. If the Bible isn't right about how we came to be and who we are, how can we trust it in other areas?[44] Peter also links this end-times spirit with Noah's day, stating that the same water used in creating the world was used by God to destroy it. But this time, Peter says, it won't be water, but rather *fire* God uses to bring worldwide judgment.[45] Forget about global *warming*. Enter global *burning*!

These three—the two witnesses, the 144,000 Jewish evangelists, and the angel who will declare the gospel the world over—all make certain the identity of the God they proclaim is unmistakable. He's the same God millions of raptured Christians worshipped and the God of the Old and New Testament Scriptures. This God's name is Jesus. And there is none other besides Him.[46]

This will be the Lord's "last call" for salvation. One final opportunity for earth's inhabitants to repent of their hatred toward heaven and their love of sin and self. There will be no more chances after this, as hearts will virtually harden to stone during the second half of the Tribulation.[47] This final, globally audible, supernatural event will effectively seal the fate of those who stubbornly refuse to believe. Skeptics often argue against theism and Christianity, claiming that if God existed, He would do something miraculous to prove it. This end-times angelic visitation will forever silence those who argue in this manner.[48] It qualifies as miraculous and sufficiently convincing. And the offer will not be repeated.

Sign #7—The Abomination of Desolation (verses 15-21)

Here, Jesus introduces a sneak preview of the second half of the Tribulation, a time when judgment is so intensified on earth that He calls it a "*great* tribulation" (verse 21). This segment will begin when a world leader, empowered by Satan himself, enters the rebuilt Jewish temple, proclaiming himself to be God.[49] His armies will also surround Jerusalem in a military conquest of the city.[50] This man will speak blasphemies against the Jewish God, ultimately demanding and requiring the whole earth to worship him.

He is Antichrist. And he will make Adolf Hitler look like Walt Disney.

According to Revelation, life on planet earth during those final 3½ years will also include wars, plagues, sores on everyone who worships the beast, rivers turned to blood, blistering heat waves, eclipses, demonic attacks on humans, supernatural signs, 100-pound hailstones falling from the sky, economic disasters, and cataclysmic climate change.

The details about the exact nature, fulfillment, and timing of these events remains unclear. However, as has been the case with previously fulfilled biblical prophecy, many of these signs may become more discernible as we come into closer proximity with them. Like distant road signs, they come into better focus as we move forward, enabling us to read them more accurately. Similarly, the closer we get to Jesus' return, the clearer our understanding of end-time events will be.

The Doppelganger Generation

In the middle of this long discourse, Jesus returns to address His disciples' original question, "Tell us, *when* will these things happen?"[51] Illustrating His answer, Jesus talks about the relationship between leaves appearing on a fig tree and the arrival of summer. When you see one happen, you know the other will happen soon. He says, "This generation [i.e. the generation witnessing these signs] will not pass away until all these things take place."[52] Like the labor pains mentioned earlier (24:8), these signs mean Christ's coming is "near, right at the door."[53]

Then Jesus gets more descriptive and historical in describing His return. Concerning the exact day and hour, He says, "No one knows, not even the angels of heaven, nor the Son, but the Father alone."[54]

He also explains, "The coming of the Son of Man will be *just like the days of Noah*. For as in those days before the flood they were eating and drinking, marrying and giving in marriage, until the day that Noah entered the ark, and they did not understand until the flood came and took them all away; so will the coming of the Son of Man be" (Matthew 24:37-39).

Of all the analogies Jesus could choose from to describe the last days, why does He land on Noah and the Flood?

One reason is because Noah lived in the "end times" of his own world and generation. Second, Noah's life and work were a prelude, leading to global judgment. Third, there were numerous observable prophecies made in Noah's time and in the generations leading up to the Flood. And finally, the state of mankind in Noah's day best illustrates what life will be like as we approach Christ's return.

Specifically, Jesus says, like in Noah's day, people in the end times will be going about their lives, doing business as usual. They'll be living for themselves without giving God a passing thought. Those in Noah's day had chosen to ignore and reject God's message of impending judgment. Likewise, His future judgment will come when unbelievers least expect it. The Flood, judgment, eternity—none of this was on their radar.

Now, Jesus didn't mention every similarity between Noah's generation and the Bible's description of mankind in the end times. But as we examine the whole of Scripture, we discover further connections linking these two "last generations." And along the way, we find there is an uncanny resemblance between Noah's generation and our own.

A Godless World

There is no fear of God before their eyes.

PAUL IN ROMANS 3:18

Few of life's mysteries are more puzzling than the sticky tension between God's sovereignty and mankind's ability to choose. How they relate and interact is a confusing conundrum—one that stretches the mind. It's one of those behind-the-scenes truths of which we're allowed only an occasional glimpse. One day this mystery will be made clear. But not yet.[1]

Possessing this gift of choice, those in Noah's world all made the same decision. They rejected the Creator—so much so that his generation was essentially devoid of God. Like He wasn't even there.[2] They had unanimously voted God off the island, eliminating Him completely from earth's equation. Humanity hung by the thread of a thin, godly family line. Though outnumbered by billions, Noah's little family is what held back God's judgment.

The days of Noah give us a sneak preview of things to come, an advance viewing of humanity in the last days. The generation witnessing the Ark's construction was a God-hating breed, and their kind will return again in the end times. Noah's contemporaries ignored heaven's message and its messengers. They carried on day after day, year after year, century after century—eating, drinking, and pursuing relationships—without even the slightest acknowledgment of their Creator or a reflection of their responsibility to Him.

They deleted God from the human hard drive, erasing Him from their collective conscience and culture. And each successive generation followed suit. Like producing like, after their own kind. Birds of a feather flocking—and sinning—together. But what did these people actually know about God? There were no Bibles or churches back then. No pastors or Christian books. No Ten Commandments. So what information did they have?

Knowing God

In the absence of a more complete revelation about God, which would come later through Moses, the prophets, and Jesus, Noah's generation still had knowledge of the Creator. Though we're unable to see God, Scripture says there are some things every person still knows about Him. He has not left mankind in the dark; instead, He has generously revealed knowledge about Himself to all mankind. In Romans 1, Paul wrote, "That which is known about God is evident within them," meaning *every person*. The reason this is true, he says, is because "God *made* it evident to them."[3] So what has He revealed, and where's the evidence for this knowledge?

The first witness God has given humankind is creation itself (Romans 1:20). Though pre-Flood earth was radically different in a multitude of ways (geography, topography, climate, and beauty), there are certain constants that transcend time. Paul said that "*since* the creation of the world" (dating back even before Noah) God's "invisible attributes, His eternal power and divine nature, have been *clearly* seen, being *understood* through what has been *made*." Several things jump out from this statement. First, every person on the planet knows there's a God simply from observing creation. Specifically, they understand He is powerful and divine. In other words, by looking at what's around us (earth, seas, sky, heavens, universe, etc.), we grasp something about our Maker. Only a powerful Creator could have brought these things into being. The heavens tell of God's glory, and the skies proclaim the work of His hands.[4] Some have referred to stars passing across the night sky as "God's travelling preachers."[5] Without saying a word, these luminaries deliver a nightly nonverbal sermon, testifying to the greatness of our Lord. Creation proclaims God's magnificent power.

But creation also provides evidence of God's divine nature as well. Through what has been made, we understand He is a *supreme* being, greater than us, and thus deserving of our attention and worship. Twice in Romans 1:20, God is given credit for creating the world. To deny or ignore this obvious reality makes us "fools" in God's eyes.[6] This disregard for their Creator-God explains the moral corruptness found in Noah's day.[7]

A highly educated man, the apostle Paul chooses his words carefully in Romans 1:19-20, using the terms "evident," "clearly" and "understood." If there is a God, He certainly would be able to provide visual evidence for His existence in a way His creation could comprehend, right? Therefore, because of this irrefutable, divine documentation, Paul says every person is "without excuse." To put it another way, no individual will ever be able to say with integrity that he or she wasn't aware there was a God. And He made sure of that by hanging a permanent, galaxy-sized sign in the sky. This insight comes naturally and is undeniable.

But there's another convincing evidence regarding the knowledge of God. This one doesn't require looking outwardly at the stars or creation. We are told that the Creator has embedded this knowledge *inside* us as well, without the need for external testimony. Romans 2:14-15 says humankind "instinctively" knows the difference between right and wrong because this knowledge is "written in their hearts" through "conscience." Like a built-in ethical alarm system, our conscience is designed to alert us regarding basic morality—things such as lying, stealing, murdering—all of which God included in the Law of Moses. It comes standard, like a computer's basic operating system, preprogrammed within us. This elementary knowledge of God is called *General Revelation*, and in spite of our fallen, sinful state, it exists in all of us.

Everyone in every era, regardless of age, gender, or race, automatically knows these things. But if that's true, how can people still deny God's existence and role in creation? Why don't they abide by the primitive moral code placed inside them? Paul anticipates this question, answering it early in his argument. He says those who deny this reality (about God and themselves) "suppress the truth in unrighteousness" (Romans 1:18). In other words, they choose to ignore it. This knowledge of God is like light, illuminating who He is and who we are. As we become aware of the basics about Him (His existence and attributes), we understand that we are His *creation*, not the Creator-God.

But because we're also simultaneously developing an addiction to self, this truth about God becomes uncomfortable and unwelcome, like sudden light in a dark room. Aware that we're fallen, we instinctively recoil from our accountability to Him. If God exists, a whole lot of issues arise—sin, death, eternity, morality, lifestyle, love, self-image, security, etc. What to do with this God becomes life's ultimate question. Who is He? How do I seek more knowledge about Him? What if I surrender and He asks me to do something risky or difficult? What if His plan doesn't line up with mine? What if He wants to be involved in the details of my life? What if He demands that I die to myself? What then?

Upgrades, Downgrades, and Denials

As these questions bombard the brain, God is seen as a threat. And so, after considering the prospect of not being in charge of our own lives, we opt for Choice B—that is, ignoring what we already know about God. We look the other way, choosing to forget Him. To use Paul's words, we "suppress the truth," following instead a path of "unrighteousness" (pursuing self and sin). Like someone trying to force a beach ball to stay under the water's surface, we attempt to drown the truth, and once it's out of sight, it's easier for us to ignore. Snuffing out the light provided, living in the dark with self becomes preferable.

This is part of that "freedom to choose" thing we spoke of earlier. Perfectly legal. Perfectly allowable. And perfectly foolish. For though there is freedom to ignore God, there is unfortunately a diminishing freedom that follows this choice. And what does this look like? Paul says the first thing to go is our perception of reality itself. Having thrown God overboard, we sail on by ourselves, left with our own (or someone else's) imagination to make sense of life and reality. So we come up with our own explanations. We pretend there's no God, again attempting to shove that beach ball underwater. But because we're an intelligent race, we realize there are inherent, self-contradictory problems with this new belief system. We know it's a boat full of holes, but we simply ignore the water seeping in. We awkwardly try explaining the origin of the universe, life, and the fact that a basic moral code (eerily resembling the Ten Commandments and Romans 2:14-15) is found in every culture on earth. In our state of denial, we strongly assert that there are no moral absolutes, even though that very statement is a moral absolute! Here comes that beach ball again, shooting up out of the water and hitting us in the face. We continue wrestling with fundamental questions like, Why is there *something* rather than *nothing* at all? But these questions cause us to think about the "God thing" again, causing more uneasiness.

Some opt for an "upgrade" in their life philosophy, transitioning from atheist ("There is *definitely* no God") to agnostic ("There *could* be a God. I don't know.") Agnostics are basically honest atheists who are willing to admit that atheism is an indefensible position. Others choose a more religious or earth-friendly philosophy, *inventing* their own god—utilizing idols of wood, stone, gold, or silver representing man or animals (Romans 1:23). They worship nature itself, the creation instead of the Creator—paying homage to Mother Earth, crystals, energy, or the "divine consciousness" in mankind. In the absence of God, they venerate some value or way of looking at life (a philosophy). Instead of worshipping the eternal God, they choose something with an expiration date.

Humans do this because we're hardwired for worship. We cannot *not* worship, no matter how hard we try. We can't help ourselves. We have to serve *something*. It's in our soul's DNA. And with no God in the picture, we're forced to fall upon "speculations" (Romans 1:21) about life in a random, blindfolded shot in the dark. A futile attempt to hit something out there, giving our fleeting, empty lives a sense of purpose. And sometimes, if we're desperate enough, *anything* will do. Unfortunately, instead of proving ourselves wise and erudite, God says we again end up becoming "fools."[8]

However, in the event people choose not to go the religious or philosophical route, they can always just default to doing whatever makes them *happy*, commonly known as hedonism or self-worship. This is where the downgrade of the slope drops dramatically. When people reach the point where they pursue self-pleasure as the highest form of existence, that's when God releases the parking brake and begins letting go. It's a choice we're free to make, and one that God honors. Treated as nonexistent, distant, irrelevant, or intrusive, God now graciously bows out from the person's life and officially "gives them over" to their own desires.[9]

With God completely out of the way, a person can then live without limitations, their only boundaries being those they set for themselves. The natural result is usually "impurity," a word Paul always associates with sexual immorality.[10] This judicial decision by God to let go is more of a sentencing, actually. "If you really want Me to leave you alone," God says, "then I will." It's a divine abandonment, and the very definition of being alone. What's left behind when God vacates a life are the passions and pursuits of a sinful heart.[11] And the possibilities are endless as these people continue descending into yet another sublevel of life without God. God abandons them, allowing them to follow whatever physical or emotional urges dominate them, including lesbianism and homosexuality.[12] Scripture describes this as exchanging the "natural function for that which is unnatural" (Romans 1:26-27), calling these desires and actions "degrading passions."

Sexuality between a male and female is natural. Homosexuality is not natural, though a mind and spirit scarred by sin may sincerely believe it to be so. However, both God and creation refute its morality and legitimacy. These individuals (for various reasons) end up embracing a lifestyle contrary to the design and order of nature itself.[13] This downward decline into moral madness and self-worship can bring about unexpected consequences, including physical disease (verse 27).

But it gets worse.

In what seems like a bottomless pit of sin, God permits those who continue in this self-worship to fall even deeper into spiritual insanity. It is at this point, with God having long since been rejected, that self and sin complete their conquest of the total person. The Creator bows out altogether, giving them over to a "depraved mind."[14] Beliefs about life, relationships, and passions are now totally absorbed into the black hole of a heart eaten up with sin-cancer. Their passions rule their reason, their lives now "filled with all unrighteousness, wickedness, greed, evil; full of envy, murder, strife, deceit, malice; they are gossips, slanderers, *haters of God*, insolent, arrogant, boastful, inventors of evil, disobedient to parents, without understanding, untrustworthy, unloving, unmerciful."[15]

This descending spiral all began with ignoring God, followed by refusing to submit to Him, producing in the end "*haters* of God." These godless people are so adept at sin now (having had so much practice), that they're actually described as "*inventors* of evil"! Further, they enthusiastically cheer on those who practice these sins.[16] It's like their vile vices have their own "fan clubs." And all this takes place even though deep down inside, buried under blankets of denial, lies the knowledge of God and His righteous standard. *That's* why Paul wrote, "They are without excuse." It's also why, in warning the Thessalonians about the end times, he stated that the Antichrist will come "with all the deception of wickedness for those who perish, because *they did not receive the love of the truth* so as to be saved. *For this reason* God will send upon them a *deluding influence* so that *they will believe what is false*, in order that they all may be judged who did not believe the truth, but *took pleasure in wickedness*."[17]

Paul gives these believers a heads-up concerning the "last days" or "last times" (words describing the period between Christ's first and second comings).[18] He tells them part of the penalty for repeatedly rejecting God is that the mind becomes numb to truth and the heart calloused to God's love found in the gospel. A hardened heart toward God brings devastating, unwanted consequences. This explains why these people are unable to believe the truth or receive His love. Instead, they embrace lies. Pharaoh is an Old Testament example of this. Defiantly dismissing God's Word through Moses, he objected, "Who is the LORD that I should obey His voice to let Israel go? I do not know the LORD...Get back to your labors!"[19] We are told that God hardened Pharaoh's heart so He could demonstrate His power and fame throughout the earth.[20] Pharaoh's heart was hardened a total of 20 times. Not even the judgments poured out during the ten plagues could soften him or break his arrogant, stiff-necked will.[21]

Pharaoh's example foreshadows those in the Tribulation who will stubbornly defy submission to God, even during horrible plagues and painful judgments.[22] But the people who lived in Noah's time were rock-hearted as well. What we see is a pattern throughout history of people defying God, even in the face of judgment. Cain. Noah's generation. Egypt. Israel. Last days. Tribulation. Willfully rejecting Jesus' salvation, which ultimately brings God's judgment.[23] And each time someone dismisses God or His truth, it just becomes easier to do it again the next time. Even believers are warned to watch for signs of developing a hard, unbelieving heart.[24] So Romans chapter 1 reveals, from a panoramic perspective, the downward spiral of those who reject God and embrace sin. Leaving God (verses 18-21) leads to idolatry (verses 22-23), leading to immorality (verses 24-27), which produces animosity (verses 28-32).

It is this continued rejection of God that triggers the gradual release of His judgment on mankind (verse 18). The consequences of this wrath include allowing the law of sowing and reaping to take its course. His anger is further revealed through abandoning men and women to their own desires, allowing them to fully pursue self and sin. Sounds like what happened in Noah's day—and what is happening in our day as well.

Ultimately, God's wrath sees its climactic end in the coming Tribulation and in eternity itself.[25]

God's Restraining Order

Clearly, in comparing pre-Flood humanity to post-rapture earth, we see that not much has changed in the human heart. It's apparent to even the shallowest observer that as a race, humanity has not improved, even when given another chance through the Flood. We are a broken creation. A ruined race. Like a car out of line, we drift to one side of the road or the other. Like dogs, we return to our own vomit, repeating our foolishness over and over again.[26] And though humanity is capable of doing good things, we still aren't inherently good, as even in our best human moments we don't measure up to God's righteous standards.[27]

That's why we need a Savior. Someone who can do for us what we're incapable of doing for ourselves. We need Someone to make us clean and declare us righteous. Someone to earn salvation for us who are wandering blindly and dead in sin. [28]

Meanwhile, godlessness continues seeping through the dam of decency, building in volume and intensity. Eventually that dam will burst, and the last wall of virtue will be breached. I believe the rapture of the church is the event that will set in motion this final deluge of ungodliness. Paul says that in the last days, the Antichrist will be revealed, a man described as being "in accord with the activity of Satan," a "man of lawlessness" and "son of destruction." He is empowered to perform "signs and false wonders." But he is not allowed his rise to power until "he who now restrains [him]...is taken out of the way." [29] I believe this restrainer is the Holy Spirit. [30] Granted, a large portion of His work in the world happens through believers because the Holy Spirit indwells all Christians. [31] His presence and power in the church does much of Christ's work here on earth. It is He who currently holds back lawlessness, hindering the global advance of sin until the final days. And He's using us in that process! However, because we're living this in real time, it can be difficult to see what a difference Christians make just by *being here.*

When Jesus first introduced the concept of church in Matthew 16, He proclaimed three powerful and fundamental truths concerning it. First, it would be built on the bedrock truth of Christ Himself. Second, *He* takes responsibility for building His church. And third, the "gates of Hades" would not prevail against it. [32] In other words, death (our ultimate enemy) has no power over those who trust in Christ because Jesus' death and resurrection conquered death and the grave! [33] Christ intended these words to encourage and comfort His disciples, especially in the later context of His crucifixion and those who would be martyred for the faith. "Even death can't stop My church!" He declares. [34]

Earlier in His ministry, Jesus described His followers as "salt" and "light," and as such they would have a preserving and illuminating influence in the world. [35] So the real questions are, "What actual good are Christians to the world?" and "What will happen when we (and the Holy Spirit in us) are taken away?" First, we must understand the distinction between the church as *institution* and the church as *authentic followers* of Christ. The church is people, not buildings or organizations. The institutional church has been blamed for many of the world's ills (bigotry, oppression, abuse of power, sexual misconduct, misuse of money, and even a percentage of wars).[36] But it's also done much good as well—establishing orphanages, founding hospitals, feeding and clothing the poor, and providing disaster relief all across the world, oftentimes being at the forefront of helping those in critical need. Individual Christians have also made significant contributions to mankind by pioneering discoveries in science, establishing higher education, and contributing to the arts and social change.[37] But don't atheists do good things too? How about people of other faiths and religions? Don't they also help make the world a better place to live? Without a doubt.[38] But as Christians, our value to the world goes beyond just doing good deeds. So how does the Spirit in us hold back evil and the spirit of Antichrist prior to Jesus' return for His bride, the church?

Among the Holy Spirit's ministries is persuading people regarding their need for salvation in Christ and of the coming judgment.[39] This work of changing hearts is His primary way of restraining sin in the world. As we who are believers talk to others about Christ, we participate in this work. Another way we participate is through our positive, godly influence in culture.

I have a friend who is one of Hollywood's most well-known stuntmen—he has worked in many blockbuster movies. I once asked him how hard it was to be a Christian in the movie industry, and his response surprised me. He told me of strong believers scattered throughout the industry. I learned about stuntmen, actors, and directors in that business who are active in Bible studies and churches. Believe it or not, the same is true in Washington, DC, where senators and congressmen serving God and country fight for decency and morality in our nation's capital. Another close friend of mine formerly played in a famous band. The after-show parties thrown for them often included plenty of opportunity for sin. But when this believer was invited, he politely declined, choosing instead to talk with these VIP fans about life, family, and Jesus.

As Christians, we may become discouraged as we consider the

ever-worsening injustices and wrongs in our world. We might even conclude God has already abandoned us, leaving all humanity to ruin. But the Lord isn't finished with our world yet. He's at work everywhere, in every nation. Wherever there are people, there are God's people and His Spirit working in and through them, impeding sin while advancing His kingdom. John's words still ring true: "Greater is He who is in you than he who is in the world." [40]

Exterminating God

Even so, Satan isn't simply going to hoist up a white flag of surrender. He's still hard at work in his planet makeover plan, transforming the world and turning it into a godless place. [41] But godlessness is more than just removing prayer from schools or taking down the Ten Commandments from the classroom. And while it is honorable to fight for virtuous values in our society, we forget that in the first century, Christians thrived under wicked and cruel Roman regimes. In a Christianized country like the United States, complacency and freedom are often bigger threats than an unfriendly government. Forbidding the mention of God in public schools or banning manger scenes in the city square are simply faint echoes of Satan's real strategy, perhaps even smoke screens or diversionary tactics. In reality, his primary battle plan calls for him and his kingdom of demonic soldiers to target the human heart. His game plan still involves doing what Paul outlined in Romans 1—getting people to ignore God. [42]

Satan prompts humanity to tell God to simply "go away." He fosters a moral climate that grows increasingly open to most anything while becoming more closed and verbally hostile to Christians and their Christ. As culture and the world become more godless, those professing faith in Jesus will become more disparaged and ostracized. The tables of tolerance will be overturned, and believers will find themselves the objects of derision and scorn. [43]

Currently we're witnessing a systematic removal of God from our culture. All over the world the Christian ideal is being choked out. It's more subtle in some areas than in others, and in some countries there is little trace of a God-consciousness whatsoever.

While relating the story of Jesus to a classroom of European teenagers, I was shocked to learn that these students had never heard of Jesus or God and had no concept of who or what He is. The most basic truths I shared were all new information to them. Though surprising, I find the same to be true in my own country among a new generation of teenagers and young adults. Many of them have grown up in evangelical churches and regularly attended youth groups and Sunday services, yet have no real knowledge of Jesus or the Bible. I find this phenomenon in my own community, where even a rudimentary understanding of God is missing. In its place is a conglomerate of miscommunicated, misunderstood facts, partial truths, and even straight-up lies about Jesus. And there's next to zero knowledge of Christianity, the Bible, and how you get to heaven...*if* it exists. Their "church" is their friend group. Their Bible is the Internet. Their pastor is social media. And their god is usually a blended mixture of philosophies and faith, or some patchwork, personal morality concerning life. Or worse, they're just deeply into themselves and well down the road of abandonment by God.

But rather than rail against the government, schools, liberalism, and the local atheist's society, the real culprit in this cultural expulsion of God is the church herself. Content to feed from the Sunday buffet of truth with our friends each week, we've remained largely silent and uninvolved in the lives of our lost friends. The reason people today know so little of God is because the Christians they know (if they know any) suddenly develop amnesia and laryngitis when it comes to communicating Jesus to them. Or they have little knowledge or skills to help someone know Christ. We think as long as we don't get hammered at the local bar or sleep around, non-Christians will notice the difference and flock to our church on Sunday to get some of what we have. We think witnessing for Jesus means reposting a conservative blog or some sentimental GodTube video. We are content to live good lives, occasionally lobbing a gospel grenade over the wall...and from a distance.

And the world continues on its downward path, unaware that a global storm is gathering.

Though Christians are, by nature, salt and light, we're also masters at hiding in the saltshaker and hitting the dimmer switch. However, as the floodwaters of godlessness continue rising, we may find that simply tossing gospel life preservers to drowning victims may be a case of too little, too late. Like a dead body, our world is slowly decomposing, and God's Spirit working through His people is all that delays the process, postponing inevitable judgment.[44]

Noah's world didn't begin without God, but it sure ended up that way.

Look around. Which way do you think we're headed?

And what are you doing about it?

A History of Violence

In the last days...men will be...brutal.

PAUL IN 2 TIMOTHY 3:1-3

It's no secret that throughout time, ours has been a civilization soaked in blood and gore. Ancient barbaric nations and people groups slaughtered one another for survival or conquest. Human sacrifices were made to Mesopotamian and Mayan gods. Medieval kingdoms created cultures of fear where criminals and dissidents alike might find themselves tortured, disemboweled, drawn and quartered, or dangling at the end of a rope. Vikings sailed across oceans and burned villages, pillaged hamlets, and raped women. We've endured civil wars, world wars, revolutions, and regional conflicts. From warring tribes to Latin American drug cartels to terrorist bombings at community events, there's hardly a place or people group on the planet that has not stared into the face of violence.

But you don't have to travel to Medellin or Detroit to find bloodshed. It's happening in our own backyards, as now even small-town residents aren't guaranteed safety from things like random school shootings.

We have sufficiently bled the ground red.

And the historical body count continues rising well into the billions. You could argue that, on the whole, we're more civilized than our barbaric predecessors. But though we may not burn people at the stake anymore, the government in some countries, like Iran and North Korea, still hold brutal public executions.[1] Some think, however, we're actually getting better, that there is less violence today than at any time in history.[2] This humanistic optimism grows out of an outdated evolutionary perspective, ultimately leading to a tunnel vision of false hope. It's analogous to Neville Chamberlain's 1938 waving of the Munich Agreement, proclaiming "Peace for our time." Within a year the United Kingdom entered World War II. In truth, we face the greatest threat when the flag of peace is proudly waving. Haven't we learned anything during all the years of recorded history?

Violence on a worldwide scale may ebb and flow, but despite our best efforts at peace, bloody conflicts still exist, due in part to the fact that evil and evil *people* exist. World peace is a worthy pursuit, but *absolute* world peace is practically impossible. In fact, it is said there have only been 268 years without war in the last 3421.[3] This means our world has experienced war over 92 percent of the time! Apparently the thirst for blood isn't limited to vampires. But where evolutionary psychology fails us, biblical truth steps in, preventing us from being lulled into complacency or being gullible to the flawed thinking that claims people are getting better. Not only are we not improving, but we're positioning ourselves for our worst moment yet. As a species, we are still fully capable of savagery, as some Eastern and Middle Eastern countries demonstrate today. And as we'll see, we Westerners like our barbarism served with a side of sophistication and science. We may be more civilized, but we are not more civil.

Not long ago while visiting El Paso, Texas, I drove along US Highway 85 overlooking the Rio Grande River. From that vantage point, I could clearly see Ciudad Juarez, Mexico. Along with the river itself, a high fence and small road are all that separate the United States from what, up until recently, had been called the World's Most Dangerous City. In 2010, a record 3000+ homicides were reported in Juarez, mostly due to drug-related cartel violence.[4] Meanwhile, across the border in El Paso, nearby mountain ridges are reportedly dotted with the homes of underling lieutenant drug lords, flaunting the fruits of their violence. These cocaine kingpins have spawned a violent culture, which borders at times on pure savagery. We view places like Juarez with disbelief and fear, much as we do other dangerous cities in Latin America and the United States. These crime capitals rise from the landscape like volcanoes of violence, erupting unexpectedly, and those in proximity to them live with a foreboding undercurrent of fear. But for most of us, this violent activity is more random than regular, usually happening "somewhere else." And this gives us a sense of security and safety. At least for now.

Nevertheless, the pages of humanity's story are stained with blood, as ours is a race all too familiar with killing and carnage. Hardly a day passes without us being bombarded with news of some form of violent behavior—suicide bombers, terrorist attacks, gang-related shootings, homicides, armed robberies, racially motivated hate crimes, or domestic abuse. So widespread is this behavior that we're hardly shocked or surprised to see it in the headlines. But in addition to the occasional news flash, we've also become a culture of curious onlookers, even developing a certain voyeuristic appetite for violence. And our demand has been heard, as media outlets expend millions of dollars producing movies, reality cop shows, documentaries on serial killers, and spousal murder exposés. Fed through our cable box and into our living rooms, we pause with morbid curiosity to be entertained by them. What we see may shock us—but apparently not enough to make us change the channel. Some argue this violent media culture inspires copycat behavior in real life.

But where does this desensitization come from? Why are we so indifferent about human violence? How did we become so *numb*? Though we make scapegoats of violent movies and video games, as culpable or complicit as they may be, they alone do not hold the smoking guns. Our tolerance for gratuitous violence can't be laid at the media's doorstep. After all, violence makes headlines, and this kind of sensational "breaking news" causes an almost guaranteed spike in viewership. Producers of news outlets, movies, and TV shows argue they're just giving viewers what they want. And as long as these programs and movies bring in revenue, they'll continue being made. However, our obsession with taking life goes even deeper, as violence seems to run in the human bloodstream itself.

Cheap Life

One of the many side effects of ignoring God is that human life is, unquestionably, devalued. If there is no God, then there is no Supreme

Maker who gives human life *intrinsic* value. There remains only *relative* value. In other words, apart from God, a human being's real worth is determined by an adjustable standard based on the laws and morals of a particular society or civilization. For example, just 150 years ago, African Americans were bought and sold like property in the United States.[5] And throughout history, human slavery has existed in nearly every culture or people group in some form. Through the domination of one race or class over another, certain ethnic groups or nationalities have been deemed less valuable than others. They're relegated to second-class status, considered inferior or subordinate in worth. The fluctuating value systems held by different cultures or groups is what supposedly justifies the domination and mistreatment of others, or at the very least, is what promotes extreme prejudice and discrimination.

But unless there is an absolute authority setting a universal standard of value for all mankind, this attitude and cheapening of life will continue. In our generation, we selectively value or devalue certain persons based on their usefulness or perceived worth. Some people are simply viewed as being more valuable. And without God in the picture, our understanding of human dignity is naturally skewed. In such cases, the rule of law and practice in society is determined either by popular opinion or whichever political party has the best lawyer.

This practice ultimately leads to an inversion of common sense and a cauterizing of human conscience. How else can we explain a civilization that vigorously defends prolonging the lives of heinous serial murderers while simultaneously fighting for the right to end the lives of innocent children? We march to keep evil men from dying while giving the unborn a death sentence simply for existing. Before the baby is even given a chance to take their first breath, we angrily defend a woman's "right" to take the life of her unwanted child. Sadly, the one advocate designed to protect and care for that life (the mother) becomes complicit in this death sentence, interrupting God's work.[6] Pro-choice advocates typically cite rape and incest as extreme examples justifying abortion.[7] Now rape is morally wrong. Always. No exceptions. And the Bible explicitly condemns it.[8] And incest is morally deplorable. Always. No exceptions.[9] But even the rapist is given rights, a trial, a lawyer, and a voice. However, who speaks for the one who cannot yet speak? Who pleads their case and defends their right to live? Abortion is controversial, and it's not going away. And neither is the devaluation of people and violence against humanity. As we saw in chapter 4, the day is coming when Christians themselves will be deemed unworthy to live.

But though politicians, activists, and the media have politicized abortion as a women's rights issue, at its core, it has less to do with a woman's choice and more to do with the issue of life itself. With God out of the picture, people become expendable because there is no divine standard to declare their worth. History teaches us that government and the prevailing spirit of the age usually decide how valuable people are. When in doubt, consider the Jews in Nazi Germany, or ask those who witnessed the slaughter of one million Tutsis in the Rwandan Genocide of 1994.[10] Both were unwanted people groups. They were considered subhuman or undeserving of life. Again, without God's standard, we are left with a sliding scale of human morality. This is why God had to tell us not to murder each another, and especially not to shed the blood of the innocent.[11] Without Him, we could eventually annihilate one another.

Over 43 million unborn children were destroyed worldwide in 2008, with over one million of those murders taking place in the United States.[12] China even practices forced abortion.[13] This is a volatile and controversial subject in our country, eliciting strong opinions on both sides. But what kind of nation writes it into law that one person's *choice* trumps another person's *right* to live? Is simply being unwanted, unplanned, and unborn justification for being terminated? This sensitive issue sharply divides us, but why? Why is a simple answer on this subject not obvious?[14]

Since 1980, more than one *billion* innocent lives have been taken, having been judged unworthy to live. Are their souls in heaven, crying out to God for justice? How many unborn will die before God avenges their blood and inaugurates the day of His judgment?[15] Have we not in just 34 years killed more unborn children than Noah's generation killed of all ages over hundreds of years? This is evidence of what happens to a civilization when divine sanctity of life is tossed out the window. It's another example of Romans 1—ignoring God and loving self.

The price tag on human life has been changed, elevating some while deeply discounting others to the bargain bin. Today, there are people who celebrate this right to end life as a *good* thing—as part of a woman's *entitlement*. Isaiah warned his own country concerning their degrading morality, declaring, "Woe to those who call evil good, and good evil."[16] It's inverted morality, and God will avenge it.

It's naive to think we won't eventually extend this devaluation to others' lives as well—targeting people by age, race, religion, physical or mental handicap—any whose "quality of life" or value to society is below our wise judgment. If it happened in the past, why couldn't it happen again? And it will. When humans of any age, race, religion, or physical condition become "undesirable," we become like those who justify genocide. Are we better than an evil dictator who kills seven million of one race when we slaughter one billion of many races? Are we now any less deserving of judgment than those whom God destroyed in the Flood?

Admittedly, the genie is out of the bottle, and the right to terminate pregnancy is protected by law. Refusing to accept a divine moral standard, we redefine when life itself begins. Sliding the scale, we again change the price tag. You would have a better chance bringing back prohibition than you would outlawing abortion. It's not going away, but neither are those who continue fighting for the unborn through legislation and helping young women see the value and beauty of human life.

In perhaps one of the saddest verses in the Bible, the author of Judges writes, "In those days there was no king in Israel; everyone did what was right *in his own eyes*."[17] In the absence of wise, godly leadership and a just government honoring the Creator, morality is auctioned off to the highest bidder and the majority opinion.

A Deeper Cut

When God gave Moses His then basic guidelines for living, He divided them up into two sections—relationship to God and relationship to man. First and foremost among those human relationships is that which exists between parent and child. Honoring father and mother was primary because God intended a child's perception of God to come from Mom and Dad. Though the command itself is directed at children, a heavy parental responsibility was implicit in that fifth commandment. Immediately after this first command regarding human relationships, God tells His people not to murder one another. He knew that violence is a sinful heart's default solution for resolving conflict, venting frustration, avenging jealousy, and satisfying anger. Jesus understood this too and expanded on the commandment, revealing a much deeper root cause for mankind's inclination for brutality:

> You have heard that the ancients were told, "You shall not commit murder" and "Whoever commits murder shall be liable to the court." But I say to you that everyone who is *angry* with his brother shall be guilty before the court; and whoever says to his brother, "You good-for-nothing," shall be guilty before the supreme court; and whoever says, "You fool," shall be *guilty enough to go into the fiery hell.*[18]

In those words recorded in the Sermon on the Mount, Jesus gives us terrific insight into God's main motivation for giving the Ten Commandments. His original plan called for doing more than just curbing bad or violent behavior. He wasn't merely demonstrating our inability to consistently obey even the most primitive moral standards. God's goal was, and always has been, to reach the *heart*. And why? Because we all have a heart problem.

In 2011, there were over 1,200,000 violent crimes in America, and every year, some 15,000 homicides are reported.[19] This includes domestic, gun-related, gang-related, robbery, and just about every other kind of violence leading to death.

From the beginning, mankind's predisposition to violent behavior was but an outward expression of a more serious inner problem. We're bent toward brutality. And while laws and consequences are good and necessary as deterrents in a civilized society, God sees more than just numbers and crime statistics. He sees the heart of humanity.

True spirituality focuses not on restricting outward actions as much as it does on changing the inner person. Our problem goes beyond our bad behavior. The trouble is with the condition of our souls. That's what the religious leadership of Jesus' day failed to understand. Their rabbinical traditions focused excessively on external behavior, ignoring the Old Testament scriptures that target the heart. [20]

That's why Jesus equates anger and devaluing other people with murder. But how are these two related? What do they have in common?

As we've seen, the very first violent act on the planet was a brutal homicide. [21] Abel's murder demonstrates that something was wrong with us from the time Adam and Eve fell into sin. Our human inclination toward violent behavior stems from a "desperately wicked" condition. [22] Cain's murderous assault on his brother was birthed out of a heart consumed with jealousy and bitterness. These quickly evolved into hatred, which led to violence. But Cain wouldn't be the last violent criminal, and definitely not the last well-known Bible character to commit murder. Both Moses and David were members of murderer's row. Applying Jesus' standard to others in Scripture, many more committed the same sin through inward anger. From God's perspective, our inner attitudes and emotions matter because they are what motivate us to do what we do, whether good or bad. And anger is most often what spawns the sin of murder.

In calling us to a higher standard, Jesus challenged the status quo of His day. The religious leaders in His generation were far more concerned that their *actions* be viewed as righteous rather than their hearts. Much later in His ministry, He would directly address these leaders, declaring,

> Woe to you, scribes and Pharisees, hypocrites! For you are like whitewashed tombs which on the outside appear beautiful, but inside they are full of dead men's bones and all uncleanness. So you, too, outwardly appear righteous to men, but inwardly you are full of hypocrisy and lawlessness. [23]

Clearly, Jesus wasn't out to gain favor from the Pharisees or win any popularity contests. He saw past their external facade due to His divine and complete reliance on the Father.[24] Christians may be tempted to think that because they support the rights of the unborn or because they're nonviolent that this somehow makes them better than others. But that's the Pharisee trap, set by Satan himself. While maintaining an outwardly respectable appearance and lifestyle, we as Christians may still harbor hidden vices and vitriolic attitudes against others. And we are *very* capable of hatred. Christians are capable of experiencing hateful moments and even seasons. This Phariseeism and hatred can cause the lines between believers and unbelievers to become indistinguishable at times. It may be expressed toward Muslims, minorities, homosexuals, and those of differing political persuasions. It can even be expressed toward other Christians—while at the same time maintaining an external illusion of spirituality and godliness.[25] And while those hateful thoughts and emotions may not get you put on trial for murder or assault, in Jesus' eyes, they do put you on the same level of those who commit such acts. It also causes you to grieve the very heart of God.[26]

Unless we recognize the source of our sin, we will forever be applying Christian Band-Aids and religious recipes to our behavior. But none of them can help the heart. Like trying to put out a forest fire with a squirt gun. In Mark 7, Jesus again addresses the core of this problem. And once again, He targets our fake friends, the Pharisees. After calling them "hypocrites" and amateurs who twist, distort, and misinterpret God's Word (verses 6-8,13), He goes for the knockout punch, telling them their real problem was that they had evil hearts (verse 15).

Ouch.

Later, Jesus' disciples privately asked Him about what He had said, prompting Him to elaborate:

> That which proceeds out of the man, that is what defiles the man. For *from within*, out of the *heart* of men, proceed the evil thoughts, fornications, thefts, *murders*, adulteries, deeds of coveting and wickedness, as well as deceit, sensuality, envy, slander, pride and foolishness. All these evil things proceed *from within* and defile the man.[27]

This is quite a list of sins Jesus gives. He says that the same heart that produces foolishness also produces fornication. Envious thoughts and evil come from the same place. So do pride and *murder*. Every one of them comes not from the big, bad world or the devil, but from *within the human heart*. "And *that*," Jesus says, "is what defiles you." As humans, our problem is not primarily an "out there" issue, but an "in here" dilemma.

It's not *them*. It's *us*.[28]

Bloodshed and violence in the world is but a symptom of the epidemic violence in the human heart. John warned the Christians of his day, "Everyone who hates his brother is a murderer."[29] Anger, hatred, and bitterness are an unholy trinity of heart-sins, as powerful as poison. And just as deadly.

Of course, we see the outward violence in our culture, and as Christians, we long for a solution while putting our hopes in all the wrong things. We've depended on government, legislation, boycotts, and political parties to restore our country to its "glory days" of low crime, high morality, baseball, apple pie, and good 'ol Mayberry family values. News flash: Those days are over. The problem is that none of those things have the power to accomplish the one thing our world really needs—changed hearts.

But because changing hearts means getting your hands dirty, many of us do our fighting from a safe distance. We still fall prey to the spirit of Phariseeism within us. We like feeling good about ourselves, especially if it makes us feel "better" than others. That's why it's easier to rant in a blog than it is to begin a meaningful relationship with a non-Christian. Easier to post a conservative political tweet than to support an unwed, pregnant teenager. Easier to rail against the evils of violence than to volunteer your time helping at-risk youth. Easier to lecture than to listen. Easier to share your opinion than to share the faith. Venting about wrongdoing may make us feel better, but it accomplishes no real change.

One of the specific reasons God sent the Flood was because of pandemic violence present upon the earth during Noah's time. In the absence of God and moral restraints, violence was unleashed. People assaulted and killed each other everywhere. With bloodshed out of control, the ground turned to crimson. And God had to wash it clean with the waters of judgment. But from a spiritual standpoint, it was merely a planet full of rotten hearts acting out their selfishness in tangible, destructive ways. Their unrestrained violence was an outward manifestation of a world full of godless, sin-drenched souls. Mankind's collective anger and subsequent aggressive actions provoked God's righteous fury. And considering the extent of their violence, what was at stake was the preservation and survival of humanity itself. God had to do something.

When discussing the problem of violence in a modern context, extreme pacifists often posture themselves as having a higher, nobler morality than that found in Scripture, especially the Old Testament. But as God demonstrates, violence is unfortunately sometimes necessary in order to stop evildoers or to preserve a nation.[30] If there were no such thing as justifiable war or forceful defense of innocent life, then only evil men would prevail. We live in a world that, despite our laws and social pressures, cannot fully protect us from hatred and violence. When humankind fails to acknowledge God's existence, respecting neither His authority nor man's, bloodshed is inevitable.

The epidemic, uncontrolled hatred and unjust violence of Noah's day invited and incited divine retribution. This magnitude of murder will only be matched by the carnage prophesied in the end times.[31] The question is, How close are we? And considering our culture of violence, both sanctioned and vilified, are we currently ramping up to judgment? The verdict is in. As in Noah's day, today's world is guilty of murder. But when will the sentence be executed? How long can we continue our brutality before God says, "Enough!" and the final fury begins?

50 Shades of Immorality

In the last days...men will be...lovers of pleasure.

2 TIMOTHY 3:1-4

If you were the devil and you wanted to destroy the Creator's design for humanity, how would you go about accomplishing that? What would be your plan? How would you implement your strategy? Following Satan's successful deception in the Garden, mankind fell, turning two pristine people into what would become a veritable planet of perverts. This became their story:

> Now the earth was *corrupt* in the sight of God, and the earth was filled with violence. God looked on the earth, and behold, it was *corrupt*; for all flesh had *corrupted* their way upon the earth. Then God said to Noah, "The end of all flesh has come before Me; for the earth is filled with violence because of them; and behold, I am about to *destroy* them with the earth."[1]

The Old Testament Hebrew word translated "corrupt" is *shachath*, which literally means "to destroy, go to ruin or decay."[2] In corrupting himself, man also ruined the earth, polluting with sin the world God provided for humanity. There's a Hebrew play on words here as Moses uses the same term describing what man had done to himself (destroy, corrupt) and what God would do to him (destroy). Translated: "You have destroyed My earth and those whom I have made, therefore I will destroy you with the earth."

This same word appears again later, describing the nation of Israel upon Moses' descent from Mount Sinai. "Then the LORD spoke to

Moses, 'Go down at once, for your people, whom you brought up from the land of Egypt, have *corrupted* themselves.'"[3]

During Moses' 40-day mountaintop seminary experience, the Israelites in the base camp below were participating in a nationwide, drunken orgy, *corrupting* themselves.[4] Sadly, it wouldn't be the last time the nation engaged in mass sexual immorality.[5]

Considering the extent of mankind's corruption during the pre-Flood days and the vile, demonic perversions we saw in chapter 1 of this book, what emerges is a portrait of planet-wide debauchery. Sex saturated every society, and people thought about it constantly.[6] It dictated their actions and ruled their relationships. It was the soundtrack to their sin-filled lives.

Satan's plan was succeeding and right on schedule. That's because he knew something about humanity. And this inside information helped him craft his strategy of corruption. But what did he know? Studying the original creation, we discover three bedrock truths about humanity:

1. Man was made in God's image—we think, feel, choose, and have capacity for relationship.

2. The male gender was created unique and distinct from the female gender.

3. Man was made for woman, and woman for man—physically and emotionally.

So if you're the highest created angel and you're expelled from heaven because of a failed coup, you now possess a venomous hatred for God and everything connected to Him. And nothing is closer to the Creator's heart than His creation and those He loves.[7] Touch the ones He loves, and you've touched the very heart of God.

Therefore this evil entity, stealthily lurking in the Garden, cleverly calculates a plan to destroy man from the very beginning. First, he plants seeds of doubt with regard to God's goodness and provision: "Did God *really* say…"[8] Following this, he tells a straight-up lie, sprinkled with truth to sweeten it up—"You surely will not die!…you will be like God, knowing good and evil."[9]

Eden's couple took the bait, devastating not only themselves but also the beautiful kingdom and creatures God made for them. Phase 1 of Satan's plan was complete. Now on to Phase 2. If you want to destroy someone, don't waste time with peripheral issues. Instead, go right for the jugular. Destroy their *identity*. In this first-ever instance of identity theft, sin now tricks Adam and Eve into believing a lie about themselves, causing spiritual amnesia. Following their sin, instead of running to their Father for help, they ran away from Him. Instead of resting in the identity He'd given them, they created substitute identities with fig leaves.[10] Instead of believing they were loved, their hearts were filled with fear.[11]

Confusion set in, causing Adam and Eve to be messed up in the head about *who they were*. There was a malfunction in their thinking. An addiction to sin was born. And this family would suffer a relapse before stabilizing.[12] Meanwhile, Satan, despite being cursed by God, didn't slither away in total defeat. Instead, his hatred only intensified, particularly toward women.[13] Corruption spread through the human race, picking up speed, replicating itself in assorted mutations and perversions. Satan's master plan was taking shape.

As we've seen, at the core of man's identity is our creation in God's image. We were made to naturally connect *with* Him and understand life *from* Him. But sin short-circuits this, *dis*connecting us from God. Unwilling to discover our true identity in Him, we're forced to make one up or find one that "fits." Enter Phase 3 of Lucifer's strategy for screwing up mankind. Further venting his loathing hatred for God, he targets our sexual identity. If Satan can confuse us about *who and what we are*, the long-term effects will be devastating. And sexuality is the perfect window through which he crawls, implanting additional questions about God's goodness and what gives us fulfillment in life.

We were created as sexual beings, and God wants us to experience our sexuality. This infinitely wise Creator also designed the *context* of sexuality.[14] Man and woman were obviously made for one another, becoming "one flesh" through sex, a beautiful outward picture of intimacy. However, Satan's agenda calls for altering this design, employing a verbal illusion identical to the one he performed in the Garden. "Did

God *really* make you for only one woman? Did God *really* create you for the opposite sex? Are you *really* a man…*on the inside*? You see, God knows you'll find real contentment if you pursue what you're *feeling*." So Satan entices humanity to seek sexual fulfillment outside of heaven's original design. He takes a natural, good desire and tempts mankind to use it in an ungodly way. Besides, physically speaking, sex feels good no matter who the sex partner is. Your body has no way of knowing whether you're on your wedding night, in a hotel room, on a business trip, or in the backseat of a car. Only your mind and spirit know this.

State of the Union

Another reason Satan targets our sexual identity is because the physical desire for sex is very strong, often ranking just below breathing and eating. Mankind's prehistoric pollution of sexuality combined confusion and curiosity laced with lust. And by Noah's day, it surely involved every kind of corruption, including homosexuality. Only a few hundred years after the Flood this corruption spread again, with Scripture calling out a twin-city civilization just south of the Dead Sea. And just like Noah, there was only one righteous man in town. His name was Lot. And according to His earlier precedent set by the Flood, God's plan called for rescuing the righteous before sending catastrophic judgment. The Lord said, "The outcry of Sodom and Gomorrah is indeed great, and their sin is exceedingly grave."[15]

The men of Sodom were described as "wicked exceedingly and sinners against the LORD."[16] Jude tells us, "Just as Sodom and Gomorrah and the cities around them…indulged in *gross immorality* and went after *strange flesh*, are exhibited as an example in undergoing the punishment of eternal fire."[17]

Exceedingly grave. Wicked. Gross immorality. Strange flesh.

This matches Paul's New Testament description of those exhibiting "*degrading passions*…their women exchanged the natural function for that which is *unnatural*, and in the same way also the men abandoned the *natural function* of the woman and burned in their desire toward one another, men with men committing *indecent* acts."[18]

Sodom and Gomorrah didn't have a "Castro District." Instead, homosexuality thrived in every quarter and neighborhood. These men were dominated by sexual desire. So intense was their lust that the entire population of Sodom (young and old) showed up at Lot's door, demanding that he release his angel visitors so they could brutalize them in a mass gang rape.[19] Refusing Lot's immoral offer of his two young daughters in an attempt to appease them (nice father!), they persisted in their compulsion to have sex with these angels. Upping the ante, they threatened to do even worse to Lot.[20] That's when God's messengers had had enough. Pulling Lot inside, they struck the men with blindness. However, so consuming was the desire to satisfy their sexual passions that they physically wore themselves out groping for the door![21]

Wow.

Blind, and still burning with lust, the inhabitants of these cities were slaves to Satan's lies and their own degrading passions. What happens next can only be described as apocalyptic—God ignites a massive explosion that rains down fire and brimstone on the valley, incinerating every human being present.[22] Condemned and reduced to smoldering ash, these "unprincipled men" who had oppressed Lot with their "sensual conduct" were made an example to future generations.[23] And why? Because sexual immorality violates God's basic design of creation.

In this sense, homosexuality is a unique sin. All sin is *not* the same.[24] God didn't flood the earth because people were telling lies or charging too much for a flock of goats. He wiped out humanity for sins that fundamentally destroyed (corrupted) the core design and creation of mankind itself. For God to obliterate the entire earth's population, their sin must have been exceptionally depraved. Those who are sympathetic to homosexuality reinterpret Scripture (and thus redefine the character of God) in an attempt to accommodate this lifestyle choice. But God has not stuttered when He has spoken on this subject.[25] We can disagree with the Bible all day long. We can say it's irrelevant to our world and age of enlightened understanding. But one thing we *can't* do is say it doesn't condemn homosexuality.[26]

Even so, this sin, when compared to stubbornly rejecting the gospel, is not the worst sin one can commit. Choosing to be a homosexual won't send anyone to hell. Choosing to reject Jesus will. There are degrees of sins carrying varying degrees of consequences. Jesus Himself spoke of Sodom to illustrate this point, clearly stating that rejecting Him brings a *greater judgment* than the sin of Sodom.[27]

However, by saying this, Jesus wasn't softening the divine stance on Sodom's sin. Knowing His Old Testament, Christ was well aware of the reasons God had destroyed it. Throughout Scripture, Sodom is portrayed as the pinnacle of depravity.[28] And Jesus mentions this city again, comparing it to the last days before His return.[29] But it's also worth restating that though homosexuality is a moral issue, it is first and foremost a distortion of God's image in us. It misrepresents mankind's identity and purpose, betraying creation itself like no other sin. If there were no God, biology and physiology would still argue against same-gender unions. And like others who struggle with sexuality, there is often a deeper search for intimacy and love involved. God made us for intense human relationship, and our sexuality plays a huge role in that. Thus when people pursue unnatural means to achieve this fulfillment, they trade their God-given identity for a substitute one.

Second, there are many reasons why people experiment with sexuality or a sexually immoral lifestyle. It's a bit more complicated than, "Hey, you're gay! Stop it!" Every person is an individual and becomes who they are for a myriad of reasons. As Christians, we unfortunately have sympathy and understanding for some sins but not others.

Third, sincere Christians tend to extremes on this issue. On the one hand, some think that condemning homosexuals is the pathway to pleasing God. Tragically, evil, misguided people masquerading as Christ's followers have given His church a black eye regarding this subject, causing homosexuals to view Christians as hateful bigots and bullies.[30] On the other hand, some Christians wrestle with accepting the Bible's denunciation of homosexuality because they have so many "really nice" gay friends. Not wanting to appear judgmental or lose their friends, they soften Scripture's harsh rhetoric. Both extremes miss the point entirely.

Fourth, we live in a fallen and morally decayed world. Though many people still respect basic moral boundaries, the cracks in society's foundation seem beyond repair. We live in a culture that by and large accepts all types of sexual expression. The spirit of the age now demands that heterosexuals accept homosexuality as normal and morally appropriate. And the controversy over gay marriage is not going away. In fact, it will gain momentum in the last days. Christians must therefore learn to live with and love their homosexual neighbors, coworkers, classmates, and friends. God isn't going to rain down fire and brimstone on the gay community in your city. Our homosexual friends and acquaintances do not have leprosy. In reality, many of them are great people. We don't have to agree with them in order to be agreeable. Christ died for them, and if God showed love to them, so should we. There is no contradiction between standing for truth and loving those who are without Christ. None. And the church must be a place where any seeker is welcome to process their spiritual journey regardless of their sin.

Finally, many genuine Christians struggle with sexual identity, including various sexual sins. God's sanctification process in us involves a sometimes *messy*, zigzag growth toward Christlikeness. Some temptations and struggles that previously haunted people may simply disappear, while others linger on, plaguing them. Virtually every Christian man I've ever known has struggled with lust.[31] Some of them, for a variety of reasons, struggle with homosexual desire. It's just their particular area of vulnerability. So the body of Christ has to help them, encouraging and equipping them to grow and be a part of a loving faith community. We must fervently love those who wrestle with their sexuality while firmly anchoring them and ourselves to the beauty of God's character and enduring biblical truth.[32]

Adult Material

But as we've seen, homosexuality wasn't the only sexual corruption in the ancient world. Heterosexual perversion was just as widespread. When discussing Satan's shades of immorality, it's easy to point the finger at someone else's sin while battling our own demons. And though we live in an ungodly world, we can't get away with simply condemning culture. The sexual experimentation of the 1960s may have spawned a revolution of carnality and eroticism, but we can't lay all the blame at the sandaled feet of the hippie generation. It goes much deeper than that, ultimately finding its genesis in a growing societal rejection of God's moral standards and a universal confusion concerning sexuality.

As in Noah's day, ours is a world that *loves* sex, and today it's used to sell everything from chewing gum to cars. Sex is everywhere. Movies. Magazines. Television.[33] Commercials. Books. Video games. And of course, the Internet, as the following statistics demonstrate:

- Pornography is a 10-billion-dollars-a-year industry, bringing in some 13 billion in 2006. That's more than what is made by the NFL, NBA, and Major League Baseball combined.[34]

- One in eight searches online is for erotic content. One in five mobile searches are for porn.

- Men are 543 percent more likely to view pornography.

- Two-thirds of college men and half of college women say viewing porn is an acceptable way to express one's sexuality.

- The mobile porn industry now boasts over one billion dollars in subscriptions.

- More than half of all boys and a third of all girls see their first porn images before the age of 13, with "sexting" increasing in popularity.

- 58 percent of men said they viewed pornography once a week or more.

- In August 2006, one survey reported 50 percent of all Christian men and 20 percent of all Christian women are addicted to pornography. In this same survey, 60 percent of the women admitted to significant struggles with lust, and 40 percent admitted to being involved in sexual sin in the past year.[35]

- Those who are self-identified as "fundamentalists" are 91 percent more likely to look at porn.

We're watching a lot of porn. At home. In our bedrooms. At work. Even at school. And the results are devastating.[36] In our sex-saturated society, even preteens are being exposed to porn, contributing to curiosity, compulsion, and even addiction in their young lives.

According to the US Department of Justice, "Never before in the history of telecommunications media in the United States has so much indecent (and obscene) material been so easily accessible by so many minors in so many American homes with so few restrictions."[37]

Pornography's impact on the degrading and devaluing of women cannot be underestimated—including, but not limited to, sexual abuse.[38] Promiscuity is so common in our culture that publicly declaring oneself a virgin now carries the same ridicule and stigma an immoral person might have suffered in another era. I witnessed a former gang-member-turned-youth worker challenge area high school students to abstain from sex on prom night. Hundreds roared in laughter, catcalling and heckling him as he attempted to share the virtues of a sex-free evening. Purity is not an esteemed value today, and those embracing it are seen as "missing out" or as weird. One-night stands, sleeping with strangers, or shacking up are all commonplace. Having sex is considered normal and often expected. Purity is not.

Today's prevailing spirit portrays women as little more than sex objects to be exploited by lust-hungry men. And apparently that's okay for some women, as long as they're considered beautiful, sexy, or desirable. A sex-obsessed culture tricks young girls into thinking their personal worth comes from making men be attracted to them. What they fail to realize is that the average man thinks more about satisfying a sexual fantasy than appreciating women for who they are. They care nothing about women as people, only as playthings. Just a means to a depraved end. It's no wonder that sex trafficking and sexual slavery are thriving, and during large sporting events (like the Super Bowl), the demand for young women spikes dramatically. In some cases, these girls are expected to have sex with as many as 50 men per day.[39] In the United States, interstate sex trafficking of minors is on the rise.[40] According to the FBI, the number of sex slave victims runs into the millions in places like Russia, Southeast Asia, and the United States. Gang rape, beatings, and unmentionable perversions are commonplace for girls trapped in sex trafficking and sexual slavery.

Sex is peddled both with the luring fragrance of mainstream media as well as the disgusting gutter stench of hardcore porn and sex slavery. It's in our world's bloodstream, and it's flowing freely. But why is this particular area of human sin so widespread? Why does it seem like our generation runs a constant, low-grade sexual fever? Why is sex so popular and enticing? Even beyond other sins?

The Naked Truth

Understanding humanity's obsession with sex means grasping why it's so appealing and alluring. Have you ever stopped to consider where your information and ideas about sex came from? What sources informed you about *who you are* and what sex *is*? Who told you about it? How did your understanding of your own sexual identity develop? Where did you get your concept of manhood, femininity, romance, relationships, sexuality, and sex itself? And how do you know if those sources are actually trustworthy? Are they "experts" on the subject, or are they merely propagating their own opinions or someone else's? How can you be sure if your ideas about sexuality are true? They may be *real*. But are they *true*? Whom can you trust? Movies? Television? The Internet? Books? Magazines? "Sexperts" with PhDs? Friends? Professors? Preachers? Family members? Yourself? How can you be confident your feelings and experiences regarding sex and sexuality are legitimate?

In understanding our sexuality, we have to go beyond just the "right vs. wrong" issue. Children understand "Don't touch!" or "Stop," but mature-minded Christians want more. They want to know *why* sex is such a big deal, and one reason is because lust and sex give us what we *want*. Products sell based on a perceived need for them, and sex is a product that will never go out of style. We're convinced we need it, and it's available to anyone willing to search for it. It's the street drug that doesn't cost much up front. And it is very stimulating.[41] Sex is appealing and pleasurable![42] It *gives* us something—a sense of fulfillment. A feeling of being wanted or loved. Mental satisfaction. Physical pleasure. Even euphoria. Dr. Judith Reisman writes, "Pornography triggers a myriad of endogenous, internal, natural drugs that mimic the 'high' from a street drug," adding it's like "mind altering drugs produced by the viewer's own brain."[43]

Hey, if it didn't feel good, we wouldn't like it or do it. Even psychologically, it can make us feel cool or experienced.

Second, sex taps into natural God-given desires. He meant it to be appealing, even designing our bodies to enjoy it. But unfortunately, our culture pressures children into facing sexual issues long before their young minds and bodies are capable of handling such information. Girls are pressured to dress and look much older than they are, accelerating their sex appeal under the guise of looking more "beautiful." Boys are exposed to information and images of naked women, forcing their prepubescent minds to process their meaning and implications. And though puberty naturally prepares the body for relationships and sex, society fast-tracks this process.

Still, attraction to the opposite sex is natural. Sexual desire and the longing to be fulfilled in a sexual relationship is a good thing. Satan knows this, and utilizing one of his trademark tactics, he tempts us to satisfy a legitimate God-given desire in an illegitimate way and in advance of God's timing. He tells us bold-faced lies coupled with harmless half-truths about sex. But like a shrewd drug dealer, he leaves out the part about "enough" never being "enough." No one lusts *once*. No one enjoys sexual stimulation and thinks, "Well, I can check that off my Bucket List. Now on to something else." Rather, the enticement of sex can become almost insatiable, and when it comes to lust, most assuredly so.[44] This explains why pornography can be so addictive. Interestingly, the Greek New Testament word for sexual immorality is *porneia*.[45]

Third, sex contributes to a genuine need for intimacy. Every person longs to love and be loved. God intended sexual union to help meet these needs. That's why being sexually active with someone greatly intensifies the relationship and connection you have with that person. Sex literally connects two bodies, making them one. You don't get any closer or more physically intimate with someone than to actually be sexually united with his or her body!

Finally, we love sex in our culture because it's one more way for our sin nature to satisfy itself through doing what God forbids. Our old nature doesn't get better over time, only worse.[46] The human heart is the source of all sexual sin.[47] As a consequence, we eventually devalue sex and redefine sexuality, our calloused consciences having dulled our understanding, turning sex into a casual thing.

So sex gives us something. It feels good. We like the temporary buzz we get from it. It's available. It can make us feel loved and satisfied. And it's a God-given desire. But when we abandon God's design for sex, this desire is exploited, and we're left to navigate sexuality using our own moral compass.

Purity or Passion?

So what are Christ's followers to do with this information? How are we to live in a sexually charged culture racing toward the end of days? What does God expect of us? Surely His counsel goes deeper than "Don't!" "Wait!" and "Okay, now go for it!" As it turns out, Scripture has a lot to say about the subject of sexuality, and 1 Thessalonians 4:3-8 addresses it directly.

First, Paul admonishes us to "abstain from sexual immorality" (verse 3). The key to this, he says, is to "learn [how] to control your own body" (verse 4 NIV). The operative word here is "learn." No one is born knowing who they are or how to navigate puberty and sexuality. No one inherently knows how to view the opposite sex or manage sexual desire. Each person has to learn this, preferably from a reliable source.[48] And there's so much involved with this learning. It begins with being around people who model what it means to be a man and woman. Some of it also has to do with environment—what you watch or are exposed to, setting up boundaries, and accountability.[49] It also relates to your circle of influence—friends, teammates, work associates.

But even when external barricades are in place, it's not enough to fully chaperone the heart. We can guard our eyes, but guarding our inner person is another matter. This is the ultimate goal and the only sure thing that can prevent our desires from wandering. And it begins with a daily decision to submit our wills to Christ.[50] Actually, it's a choice we must make many times throughout the day for many reasons. A heart wholly yielded to God is the best defense against lust. If we delight ourselves in God—willfully and mentally—He will put His desires in our hearts.[51]

Overcoming this struggle continues through recognizing temptation and weaknesses. Every person has specific and sometimes unique areas of susceptibility to sin. Knowing yourself well helps identify those areas, recognizing them when they appear. This way you don't get blindsided or find yourself overcome with reoccurring disobedience. It's one thing to get wounded while fighting and quite another to be taken out by sniper shot. Know where and when you're vulnerable so you can face your battle with honesty and preparedness. And know when to call for backup through healthy accountability.

Third, fill your mind with thoughts that promote purity. Choose to dwell on things that help, not hurt you. It's a life principle that what fills our thoughts will form our character and influence our actions. This is important when it comes to sexuality because you won't engage in immoral activity unless you first *think* about it, right? And in those other moments when your body elicits an urge, your mind can control it because you're submitted to Christ.[52] That's part of what Paul meant by "control your own body." Allowing God's thoughts (Scripture) to occupy your mind brings peace and helps you overcome sin.[53] When addressing this subject, Jesus focused on the heart and mind.[54]

Paul says that exercising such control contributes to our sanctification and honors our bodies. He contrasts this with how those who don't know God live in "lustful passion."[55] "Don't take advantage of one another, sexually robbing and cheating others in this way," he adds.[56] Impure sexual conduct matters because it betrays God's design. It also invites His discipline. For believers, sexual purity isn't just a good idea, it's a *calling*.[57]

Removing God from the context of our sexuality results in being ruled by our own passions. That is exactly what Paul warned Timothy about regarding the end times. In his last-ever letter, he wrote, "Realize this, that in the last days...men will be lovers of self...without self-control...*lovers of pleasure* rather than lovers of God."[58] The phrase "lovers of pleasure" combines two Greek words—*phileo* and the word from which we get the term *hedonism,* or the belief that pleasure is the highest good man can achieve. It's the philosophy that says, "If it feels good or personally gives me pleasure, then I will pursue it and enjoy it. If it delights or gives me enjoyment, it *must* be good." That's how unbelievers will live in the last days, according to Paul. The pursuit of personal pleasure will rule their minds and actions, leading to every variation of immorality.

Specifically, homosexual relationships attempt to mimic God's original design for humanity. Sexually, they imitate creation's model, substituting biblical intimacy with a counterfeit experience. According to ancient Jewish rabbis, homosexuality was practiced worldwide before the Flood. These esteemed teachers claim that marriage contracts were written between homosexuals in Noah's generation, with songs even composed for such occasions.[59] If they're right, that's something that hasn't been legitimized in any civilization since before the Flood, and could add nuance to Jesus' words about those in Noah's day being "given in marriage."[60] These rabbis also wrote that once homosexual marriage was officially recognized, this served as the trigger to unleash God's judgment via the Flood.

The corrupt generation of Noah's day incited a sexual mutiny, producing a planet immersed in sensuality. This same obsession with sex will also characterize humanity at the end of the age.[61] Satan remains the great counterfeiter. A master manipulator of truth. A twister of reality. And nowhere does this specialty shine more brightly than when it comes to sexuality. By definition, when you fall for a lie, you don't *know* it, and thus believe you're sincere and right. That's what Satan has done to our global consciousness regarding sex. His agenda is on course and going according to plan.

Tragically, we now live in a world that celebrates same-sex marriages and shames those who uphold God's design, It's a world that views those who "parade their sin like Sodom"[62] as being courageous heroes.

While it is impossible, irresponsible, and foolish to make predictions regarding the exact timing of the last days, we do appear to be seeing storm clouds gathering on the horizon. A planet that is intoxicated with its own sexual pursuits and perversions is a sure sign we're closer now than ever before.

Difficult Days

...holding to a form of godliness, although
they have denied its power...

<small>PAUL IN 2 TIMOTHY 3:5</small>

Some things in life happen all at once. Overnight. In the blink of an eye. Like lightning, they strike in an instant. You notice such things. They catch your eye and captivate your attention. You can mark them by date. Like the birth of a child or a college graduation, you document them, capturing the moment with a photograph. They're described as events or happenings. They're obvious. Clear and undeniable.

But other things in life are not so discernible. They sneak up on you. They go unnoticed because they happen gradually over time. Little by little, their progress is so slow you may not observe any change. And unless you have a trained eye, such change goes undetected. You wake up one day, and suddenly you're getting dressed for your daughter's high school graduation. You turn around, and your son is driving. You wonder how those college years passed so quickly, or how you could have gone from being thin to being "not so thin" over time.

We're not so good at observing the microchanges that take place in our lives. Because of this, we are often oblivious to the minor or gradual transformations—both healthy and unhealthy—that take place around us or through the years.

No one today considers Harvard University to be a conservative heavyweight or defender of Christianity, but it wasn't always this way. This well-known school owes its origins to the gospel of Jesus Christ. In fact, most Ivy League schools were established primarily to train ministers. And Harvard's first presidents insisted there could be no true knowledge or wisdom without Jesus Christ.

Harvard's "Rules and Precepts" adopted in 1646 included the following essentials:

> Every one shall consider the main end of his life and studies to know God and Jesus Christ which is eternal life...every one shall seriously by prayer in secret seek wisdom of Him...in reading the Scriptures twice a day that they be ready to give an account of their proficiency therein, both in theoretical observations of languages and logic, and in practical and spiritual truths...[1]

Within 50 years, Yale was founded, partially because some believed Harvard's spiritual climate was not what it once had been. Other schools followed—Princeton, Dartmouth, Columbia, William and Mary, Rutgers, and Brown. Virtually every institution founded in the American colonies prior to the Revolutionary War was established by some branch of the Christian church.[2] However, none of these institutions are known today for churning out gospel preachers. So how did these schools go from training ministers to being citadels of theological liberalism? Easy answer.

Gradual change over time.

My wife once sat on the board of a national Christian organization dedicated to the spiritual development of young women. By the time she took her place on the board, there was no spiritual emphasis whatsoever in the organization. There weren't even any young women! Just elderly ladies doing crafts and water exercises in a big pool. Before long, even that was dropped. The organization lost its purpose and identity, and eventually its local office in our city shut down.

Like the aforementioned Ivy League schools, it had gotten to the point that it hardly resembled its former self.

But this isn't just the pattern of Christian universities. It's the pattern of faith itself. Through some 1656 years, we can trace the rebirth of faith through Adam's son, Seth, all the way down to the last man standing, Noah. But something happened along the way to this legacy of faith.

Why did godly people basically become extinct by Noah's time? The Bible doesn't list a full genealogy of the human race, but only those relevant to the story God is telling. Still, we know there was a strong line of faith from Seth to Enosh, all the way down to Enoch. But surely others in their lineage would have embraced the faith as well. It wouldn't make sense that out of these family lines, only a single person from each generation would embrace the faith. There must have been others—wives, sons, and daughters—who called upon the name of the Lord. We just don't know who they were and why their legacy died off.

Though we cannot be certain as to the exact nature of this faith departure, we do nevertheless see an emerging pattern—humanity begins well, but falls away over time. By the time Noah came on the scene, the godly line of humanity had been whittled down to a handful of people. Gone were the offerings of sacrifice. Lost were the practices of prayer and seeing children as gifts from the Lord.[3] Faded away was the lifestyle of devotion to Yahweh. And gradually, virtually undetected, fathers failed to pass on the faith to their sons. Mothers neglected to nurture their daughters. And with godlessness exponentially spreading across their world, it became easier to let it slide and go along with the flow of culture. And the line of Seth shrank down to a faithful few.[4]

This falling away may indeed have been due, in part, from the overwhelming pressure and influence of civilization becoming progressively more ungodly. Like water to a sponge, people become more and more absorbed into their culture. Swept into sin by an irresistible undertow, they simply *fell away*. But Noah's life stood in stark contrast to the people in his world. In the midst of a hurricane of sinful activity, he remained anchored to a rock-solid hope.[5] And as the ratio of wicked to righteous greatly increased, judgment became inevitable.

The Departed

According to Paul, during the coming Tribulation, a great "apostasy" (aggressive departure or revolt) will occur.[6] This climactic event will involve the Antichrist, who will make a pact (covenant) with Israel at the beginning of the Tribulation. He will be sympathetic to the Jewish people, thus giving the impression that he is a man of faith.[7] But at the midpoint of this seven-year period, he will break his covenant by desecrating the temple. In what Scripture labels the "abomination of desolation," the Antichrist will enter the rebuilt Jewish temple and proclaim himself to be God.[8] This Satan-energized son of destruction will oppose and exalt himself "above every so-called god or object of worship, so that he takes his seat in the temple of God, displaying himself as being God."[9] That act will be the ultimate snub against the Jewish God. It will be Satan's final attempt to sit in the place of God. And Antichrist's right-hand man, the miracle-working False Prophet, will command the earth to make an image to the Beast (Antichrist), which he will cause to come to life, speak, and even kill those who refuse to worship the Antichrist.[10]

"This temple abomination," Jesus tells His Jewish brothers living in those days, "will be your cue to RUN!"[11]

However, Paul also says that in the last days we will see another apostasy, this one prior to the rapture and more of a process than an event. "The Spirit explicitly says that in later times some will *fall away* from the faith, paying attention to deceitful spirits and doctrines of demons."[12]

As in the days of Noah, there will be an abandonment of authentic faith. Some today pray fervently for revival in the church, and there may indeed be a final awakening in the body of Christ in the latter times. However, no such revival is mentioned or prophesied in Scripture. What *is* guaranteed, however, is that a growing departure from the faith will occur. Paul uses this term, "the faith," to refer to the basic body of doctrine "once for all delivered to the saints."[13] The content of this faith is found in the Scriptures, and it is complete. There is nothing to add to this body of knowledge, including accounts of supposed visits to heaven or new revelations.[14] Believers are admonished to watch out for those who would (even unintentionally) deceive them with a spoken *message*, something *written*, or even with a spirit of *thought*, especially as it relates to the end times.[15]

Paul's prophecy regarding apostasy is directly from the Holy Spirit Himself, who warns us of "deceitful spirits." One of the great threats to a church or a Christian is that departing from the faith happens, as it were, in centimeters, not kilometers. It's ever so subtle, so undetectable that it may take years to notice a measurable change. That's why he calls these spirits "deceitful." By definition, when you're deceived, you aren't aware of it, so much so that you may even deny it has happened. It comes not with a blatant lie, but rather with slight nuances that chip away at the foundation of biblical truth.

The Spirit also says some drawn into this apostasy will pay attention to "doctrines of demons." We've seen some of Satan's overt attempts to corrupt mankind in general, but this particular apostasy concerns those *inside* the church. These demonic doctrines do not involve the temptations toward godlessness, violence, or immorality, but rather are *religious* in nature. Satan is perfectly happy with people being religious. Religion is one of his greatest weapons, used to keep people from experiencing a close relationship with Christ. It's all about effort and working toward achieving things and earning God's approval. And it's everything Jesus died to save us from.[16] But there is no act, however religious it may appear, that can improve our position before God. Jesus already earned it all for us. We only need to rest and abide in His provision. As long as people think something they *do* can affect their standing before God, they will continue to fail and remain enslaved to a works mentality.

Paul warned Timothy about men who add religious rules to faith in an effort to appear more spiritual. He mentioned two ways they do this: renouncing marriage and self-denial through diet. The apostle had already informed the Colossians that rule-keeping, especially as it involves diet and religious laws, has zero power to make us more holy. It was a deception, for appearance only, making people think they were wise and spiritual.[17] He combated this belief by declaring that all foods were "created to be gratefully shared in by those who believe and know the truth."[18] The direct implication was that these rule-makers only *thought* they knew what they were talking about when it came to matters of faith. But Paul exposed them for who they really were—apostates with a dulled understanding, promoting heresy.

Paul also declared where such erroneous teaching comes from. He said these people were "seared in their own conscience as with a branding iron."[19] Conscience is the part of us that distinguishes between right and wrong. It's like a sentry standing at the gate of our mind. When information or a choice is presented to a person, his conscience helps him to know whether it's right or wrong. But some people will overrule their conscience because they see the truth as either too simple or insufficient. To them, the simple truths about God as Creator and Christ as Savior are too elementary. And because they see themselves as intellectuals, they reject those truths.

Paul had firsthand experiences with such people.[20] That's why he urged the Corinthian believers not to be deceived away from "the simplicity and purity of devotion to Christ."[21] It's also why he made sure they understood the profound depth and wisdom found in that simplicity.[22] So truth is sometimes rejected because it appears too simpleminded.

But God's truth also happens to offend some people. And there are others who don't like it because it threatens their lifestyle.[23] Religious teaching can comfort and ease the soul, and even many doctrines of Christianity are meant to provide assurance and consolation. But Christ's teachings were not always so tame and peaceful in nature. Some of His sayings were hard to accept.[24] Other times His words were demanding, causing many of His disciples to depart and not walk with Him anymore.[25]

So when presented the unfiltered truth of God, some choose to either suppress it or season it to better suit their tastes. In these ways the conscience becomes "seared" as with a branding iron. When Paul spoke of such searing, he was referring to the custom of cauterizing wounds, as was done when a soldier was wounded in battle or when a physician treated an open wound. Applying a hot iron to a wound burned the nerve endings, effectively making them numb and insensitive to touch. Thus, by rejecting or modifying God's truth, people essentially numb themselves. They become insensitive to God's truth and end up inventing their own beliefs, coming up with whatever is suitable to their own preferences.

The Ultimate Selfie

One mark of the apostasy that will take place during the latter days is that people will add to or alter the Word of God. These modifications will be made because people are calling into question the trustworthiness of God's Word itself. So we must watch out for those who tamper with or omit specific doctrines found in the Scriptures. But that's not all that will happen—there's more. In a follow-up letter to young Timothy, Paul further describes what this falling away will look like:

> Realize this, that in the last days difficult times will come. For men will be lovers of self, lovers of money, boastful, arrogant, revilers, disobedient to parents, ungrateful, unholy, unloving, irreconcilable, malicious gossips, without self-control, brutal, haters of good, treacherous, reckless, conceited, lovers of pleasure rather than lovers of God, holding to a form of godliness, although they have denied its power; avoid such men as these (2 Timothy 3:1-5).

Paul calls these times "difficult," referring to an age during which, once again, like Noah's day, self-gratification is king, both inside and outside the church. The first and most dominant characteristic of these people is that they are "lovers of self." They think very highly of themselves and of their opinions. And this cornerstone character flaw will color all else that follows.

Enamored with their own egos, these people will begin blazing a path toward apostasy. Even the faith they profess exists to serve self. Feel-good preachers will peddle self-love as a high virtue, even though such teaching is nowhere taught in the Bible.[26] Our greatest need today is not for a "good self-image," and yet that seems to be driving a lot of the Christian message today. Our best life is not achieved through pumping up our self-esteem, but by seeing ourselves as we are—sinful before God, and yet *deeply loved*. It is only then that His grace and salvation can be understood and appreciated. Only then do we grasp our incredible worth in God's eyes.[27]

The greatest gift in life is embracing the mega-love God has for us. This naturally produces a love for Him and others, not a romance with our own selves. On the contrary, our motto should match John the Baptist's: "He must increase, but I must decrease."[28] Self-love is the pinnacle of depravity and the cause for more relational conflict, division, and heresy in the church than anything else. It's also a clear sign of latter-days apostasy.

Those caught up in this apostasy will also love money (which they, no doubt, will spend on themselves). Materialism. Stuff. Things. Possessions. And every bit of it to prop up the facade of self even more. They will never be content. Or satisfied.[29] This is not to say Christians should take a vow of poverty or turn down a higher-paying job. Wealthy believers, both in Scripture and today, are among the most generous and godly people alive. Having riches isn't the issue. Riches having *you* is the issue. Money is a great servant, but a cruel master. And under the control of a self-centered heart, it leads to all sorts of evil.[30]

Further, the people of the latter days will be arrogant. They will brag. A lot. Mainly about themselves—what they have, what they've done, or who they know. They will constantly one-up each other or put others down while simultaneously exalting their own status. And they won't like authority, especially the parental kind. Any attempt to thwart self-rule will be met with opposition. This defiant attitude will follow them into the classroom, on the job, at home, and at church. In fact, we already see this happening today. When was the last time you heard someone say they were "under the authority" of their pastor?[31] Sounds a bit *cultish*, doesn't it? And yet few consider themselves to be under any type of spiritual supervision, choosing to handle all their own spirituality…by *themselves*, of course.

Because of their innate pride, those who gradually fall away will find it hard to be truly grateful. Inwardly and perhaps outwardly as well, they will be indecent and unholy. Their disregard for God and pursuit of self-gratification will cause their love for others to grow cold, just as Jesus predicted.[32] And so, they will just keep pleasing self. They won't be reconciled in relationships, and they will refuse to change their attitude about themselves. They are never to blame; instead, they will constantly accuse others. They will take pride in saying, "Haters gonna hate," an excuse allowing them to say and do whatever they want without shame or caring what others may think or say. Their reckless, conceited lifestyle will cloud their thinking, making them blind to their own faults while they point out the faults of others. They will be brutal, always ready for a savage attack, eager to verbally tear someone to shreds. "Malicious gossips" is the Greek word *diaboloi*, from which we derive the English word *diabolical*. It's also the same word used to describe the devil 34 times in the New Testament. They will despise that which is good and decent.

Paul concludes his laundry list by describing this last-days generation as being "lovers of pleasure rather than lovers of God." Their deepest affection will lie in doing only that which gives them enjoyment and satisfaction. Giving will not be their forte. Instead, they will consume. Their default mode will be toward that which feeds the insatiable me-monster within them. It will demand attention at all times. Nothing will trump self. It will reign supremely from its seat of authority in the throne room of this fortified castle. Again, "lovers of pleasure" refers to hedonism, or the belief that personal pleasure is the highest form of good. And though the word may not be tattooed on one's arm, hedonism nevertheless runs in the bloodstream. This attitude says, "It's all about me." Subconsciously, to these persons, all things exist for one reason—to please self. A momentary satisfaction. A temporary thrill or short-lived elation that lasts until the next feeding. And because the love of self and pleasure is all-consuming, there is no room in the heart to love God. No room on that throne for two.

Meanwhile, on the surface, these people may appear to be admirable folks. They won't necessarily flaunt their wickedness for all to see. In fact, they may be religious people, possibly church members. They will "hold to a form of godliness, although they have denied its power." They will know the drill. They will appear respectable. They will speak the Christian lingo, and will fake it with the best of them. But like the Pharisees of Jesus' day, they won't even know that they don't know. So deluded will these counterfeit Christians be that they'll think they're pretty righteous, especially when compared to "really bad" people. But their godliness will be an illusion, a self-induced hoax. A religious ruse. An inner mechanism projecting a phantom image of themselves. The person they believe themselves to be will merely be a ghost. An apparition. A mind-generated myth. They will morph themselves into whatever kind of "Christian" they need to be.[33] They will be shape-shifters, chameleons who adapt to their environment as their self-preservation and pleasure dictate.

They will be fakes. And hypocrites of the worst kind.

And they will be everywhere.

In the last days, some in this religious rogues' gallery will posture themselves as teachers, desiring disciples of their own. They will prey on the weak, especially women, capturing their attention and captivating their minds and hearts with false teachings. But even though they fill their lives with learning, neither they nor their followers ever come to a real knowledge of the truth. They will seek more religious education, but will be prevented from receiving the knowledge of God.[34] Simple, plain, biblical truth won't be enough for them. They will feel compelled to go beyond God's Word, continually digging elsewhere but finding only fool's gold. Always learning, never knowing. Reading books and writing blogs but never getting it right. Posing as intellectuals or even as sincere, devout believers, in reality they will be mere facades. Like stage sets for a play, they will seem real, but there will be nothing real behind them. Just a shallow veneer of spirituality.

Jesus encountered their kind in His day, prophesying about them. "Just because someone calls Me Lord doesn't mean they're truly Mine or that they're going to heaven," Jesus said.[35] Apparently, talk will still be cheap leading up to the last days. And in fact, these people will not only talk a good game, they will also act it out as well. Some will even make "prophecies," appear to cast out demons, and seem to perform many miracles.[36] But the Lord has a special word on judgment day for these people who profess Him as Lord and do good deeds in His name: "I never knew you; depart from Me, you who practice lawlessness."[37]

Christ also said that while on earth, believers and unbelievers will coexist in the same spiritual family (the church). And it will be hard to distinguish one from the other. But at the end of the age, the sheep and the goats will be separated—the sheep to eternal life, and the goats to eternal fire.[38]

The most tragic commentary about these people is that they thought they were Christians all along. Apostasy is usually subtle, coming from even well-educated people. But alarms should go off in your head whenever a professed believer disputes the Word of God, the deity of Christ, His substitutionary atonement, or His bodily resurrection. These are nonnegotiables of the faith.

Beauty and the Buffet

Falling away from the faith usually goes hand in hand with falling in love with ourselves. And even churches are vulnerable to this apostasy. In a sincere attempt to reach our culture, churches can become obsessed with giving their attendees what they want over what they need, creating a consumer-driven culture within. Convenience and comfort become king as those who attend church come to expect certain amenities and the same perks that are available at the local mall. From shuttle buses to coffee shops and even ATMs, more and more churches are expending tremendous effort toward accommodating the consumer. They even provide "venue menus" for those who prefer different styles of worship.

Many churches have become ecclesiastical superstores with a department and aisle for everyone, regardless of personal taste or preference. Like the federal government, they have programs in place to meet every need of the buying public. They have become experts at dispensing religious goods and services. They produce Broadway-style plays and Disney-like productions, all with the idea of entertaining, educating, and getting more people into the building. And more people means they might be able to pay off that huge building or even build a bigger one. They have multimillion-dollar sound systems, crystal chandeliers, state-of-the-art television production studios, and of course "green rooms" where the "talent's" favorite snacks are provided. And if they're really good at their Sunday production, the church may get a "tithe-tip" from the 20 percent of members who do that sort of thing, either out of obligation or sincere love for God.[39]

Obviously, what I have just described is not true of every contemporary church. But in many circles it is these kinds of things that are modeled to us as being necessary to become a successful church. Some of these churches even franchise themselves so others can have the privilege of being like them and wearing their "brand."

As we draw closer to the latter days, I fear we've lost the essence of vintage Christianity. We've become domesticated and tame, many churches having grown into corporate giants, landowners, and multi-million-dollar institutions "providing a service" for their members and the community. "Helping you; helping others" is their motto. But are we really tending the sheep or merely entertaining religious goats? We spend more time practicing music transitions than praying. More time on ambiance and lighting than sacrificially serving one another. We pour millions into buildings and presentations instead of people. We forget we are a body with members, not a business with a board of directors. A living organism, not an organization. We are more concerned with filling our facilities with more consumers than doing the one thing Jesus commanded us to do—*make disciples*. We hire marketing consultants to give us direction instead of desperately depending on the Holy Spirit and prayer. We elect wealthy men with successful businesses to our boards, often ignoring men full of faith and the Spirit. We have CEOs instead of shepherds. "Directional leaders" instead of pastors. What have we become?

Several years ago I received an urgent phone call one Monday evening. A friend called to say that Ellen, a precious 13-year-old girl who had been attending my youth ministry, had been taken to the emergency room.[40] This beautiful young woman was the product of a broken home. Her mother was struggling to raise Ellen and her little sisters as best she could. But mom also had other issues as well, not the least of which was making poor choices when it came to men. Having gone through several boyfriends, her most recent selection was a real loser.

Fortunately the hospital was just a mile or so from my house, so I was able to jump into my car and get there immediately. Running into the emergency room, I asked the nurse where Ellen was, and she pointed down the hall. Walking quickly past the small rooms, I glanced into open doors, looking for her, but she was nowhere to be found. Of the three trauma rooms in use, one was occupied by a pregnant mother, another an old woman, and the last, an elderly man.

Returning to the nurse's desk, I once again asked where Ellen was being treated. And she again pointed down the hall, whereupon I politely asked her to be a bit more specific.

"Room 2," she replied.

"But I already went there," I explained. "There's an old woman in there."

"That's the room, sir," she stated bluntly, a little more irritated this time.

Confused, I returned to the room, slowly peeking inside the doorway. The woman was sitting up on the bed, clothed in a traditional hospital gown. Her hair was disheveled and her eyes were swollen shut. Her face was blooded and bruised, puffed up nearly twice its normal size.

It was Ellen.

As others began arriving, I soon learned about what had happened. The boyfriend had become upset with Ellen's mom and started abusing the single mother of three. Ellen stepped in to protect her mom, and that's when he turned his anger upon the 13-year-old, beating her repeatedly until she finally went limp. He fled, and eventually the police and ambulance showed up. And that's how a beautiful little girl like Ellen ended up in Trauma Room #2.

That was more than 20 years ago, but I can still vividly recall the sight of young Ellen sitting on that bed. I can still see her face as she tried peering through her swollen eyes. I had missed her the first time, mistaking her for someone else. I didn't recognize her because she didn't look *anything* like herself.

If we could transport ourselves back to the first century and attend the church at Colossae, I wonder what we would see. Walking into that house church on a Sunday evening, we'd likely find people who had just come from work, since Sunday was the equivalent of our Monday workday. We'd see all types of people—different demographics, races, and classes. Old and young, rich and poor. All gathered together to be with those who loved and supported them. They would eat together, pray, hear from a teacher or pastor, remember the Lord's death for them, probably sing a song, and go home. But it wasn't so much what they did as it was the reason for their gathering. They didn't come together merely because it was "time for church." They did it because they really needed one another. They longed for fellowship and rest from a hostile world. They did it because they were hungry to hear what God would say through His apostles or His written Word. They didn't come to be entertained, but to be with their spiritual family. To be equipped and built up. It was simple and without fanfare. All the focus was on Jesus.

Were we able to attend such a gathering as that, would we walk away wondering if we had really been to church? Would we subtly judge their lack of preparation or criticize their crude accommodations? Would we snub their music or lack thereof? Would we be bored at the speaker's unpolished presentation? Or turning the tables, what if an average believer from that same Colossae church were to attend one of our churches today? What would she say? How would she feel? Would she be welcome? What would her impression be, not of the singing performance on stage or the presentation of the pastor, but of the "spirit" of the church itself? Would she *recognize* the church? Would she leave confused or perhaps even grieved?

This is not to exalt first-century believers to sainthood or those early churches to some romanticized status. Nor is it to discount or demonize today's use of creativity, technology, humor, or professional excellence in the church.[41] It's not about form or type of service or whether we use high-definition projectors or digital cameras. Our real dilemma lies in the fact that the church is in danger of losing her soul. Compared to what we see of the church in Scripture, she has become practically unrecognizable in some places.

What would happen if we just gathered on Sunday and did the simple things? What would happen if, for one year, we didn't entertain or put on an elaborate multimedia, multisensory presentation? Odds are that some people—or maybe even many—would stop coming. That's because we've created a hungry beast that now cries to be fed. By focusing on giving people what we think they want instead of what they need, we've birthed a Christian culture of *takers*. They've come to get the freebies, the spiritual handouts they feel they're entitled to.

And we shudder to think what would happen if the sound system were to go down or we ran out of coffee.

Simply put, we have become very good at *doing* church in our culture and have forgotten how to simply *be* the church, specializing in the things that really matter.

Paul warned Timothy,

> The *time* will come when they will not endure sound doc-
> trine; but wanting to have their ears tickled, they will accu-
> mulate for themselves teachers in accordance to their own
> desires, and will turn away their ears from the truth and
> will turn aside to myths. [42]

Paul uses the same word, "time" (age, era of time), that he used earlier in his letter, referring to the "difficult times" describing the last days (2 Timothy 3:1). One of the signs of the coming apostasy will be a departure from sound doctrine. In this age that flatly rejects uncomfortable truth from God's Word, Christians will be tempted to "modify" their belief systems to accommodate their culture and pop-ular thought. The pressure to soften certain biblical truths or redefine them will become greater. As sound doctrine becomes more unpopu-lar, so will those who embrace it. Christians, churches, and even whole denominations will continue to turn truth into myth, "tickling" peo-ple's ears. Paul had earlier described those who stray from the truth, referring to their lifestyles as "contrary to sound teaching." [43] These people want a church that always makes them feel good.

Paul's warning applies to armchair philosophers and wannabe theo-logians who advocate doctrines that are different from those found in Scripture. Their teachings will lead others into ungodliness. These people, obsessed with controversial topics and theological minutiae, will debate and argue over every point—much like the many supposed Christian bloggers today who posture themselves as theologians and Bible experts. Paul flatly states that such people are "conceited and [know] nothing." [44] Such evil men and imposters "will proceed from bad to worse, deceiving and being deceived" as we approach the end times.[45] But unlike the unbridled carnality so clearly evident in the world around us, this turning away from God is subtle and deceptive, and in the faith community, it is a telltale sign of the last days.

The call away from the edge of apostasy not only means guarding sound doctrine and making disciples, it's also a call for the church to simply be herself. To return to what Jesus called her to do. To recapture her original beauty, that which is simple, deep, innocent, and pure.

In reality, we don't need a time machine that enables us to visit the early church. We can encounter her (along with all her imperfections) through the New Testament. We can also recapture the heart of Jesus for His bride. That's the ideal we strive for—to be wholly His. To become like Him in all respects. And anytime we get too caught up in building up and maintaining the church, that's when it's time to rethink our purpose and existence.

Jesus still loves His church. He cares passionately for her. And He wants to help protect her from those who would harm her, abuse her, or disfigure her, altering her original beauty.

"Difficult days will come," Paul predicted. And this departure from doctrine and the faith will characterize the last days leading up to Jesus' return.

The remedy, Paul says, is to keep growing and being convinced by the truth found in the Scriptures, which is "profitable" and able to make you "adequate, equipped for every good work."[46]

And that's good medicine.

Coming with the Clouds

The time is near.

<small>REVELATION 1:3</small>

A few years ago, while visiting a small English town, I had the privilege of having lunch with a group of retired gentlemen and ladies. After being seated beside this one particular woman, we struck up a conversation, and I soon discovered it was her birthday.

"How old are you, ma'am?" I asked.

This question caused everyone at the table to look up from their freshly poured cups of English tea.

"One hundred years, today," the woman said.

"Wow," I said, not knowing whether to shake her hand or ask for her autograph. Instead, I chose to probe further, inquiring, "So what are some of the things that stand out in your mind over the past one hundred years? What are your most vivid memories?"

Delicately stirring her tea, the elderly woman thought for a moment and then matter-of-factly replied, "Well, I remember when German bombs fell on our town back in 1940." Then she looked at me, stating in a proper English accent, "But I guess one of my earliest recollections would be when the *Titanic* went down. I remember that one rather well."

Like a schoolboy meeting a sports legend, for the next 30 minutes I sat in silence, listening intently to the stories this dear old woman recounted. It was a lunch I never forgot, though none of her stories blew me away like her recollection of the *Titanic*.

The sinking of this ship was one of the greatest maritime disasters in human history, and since then, the name *Titanic* has been synonymous with tragedy. On April 10, 1912, what was then the world's largest ocean liner left Southampton and began her maiden voyage across the North Atlantic with over 2200 souls on board. Her captain, Edward Smith, was a seasoned sailor, and it was rumored he would retire following this journey. Four days into the voyage, everything was going as planned. Passengers were enjoying themselves, doing what people do on a luxury liner—eating, drinking, playing, relaxing. The skies had remained clear and the seas calm, making for a tranquil and uneventful trip. The last thing on anyone's mind was danger. In fact, the opposite sentiment was present in the minds of *Titanic's* 1316 passengers, all secure and confident given the ship experts' proclamations that the vessel was "unsinkable." But seven-year-old Eva Hart had a different experience. Having been originally booked on another ship, weather had prevented the Hart family from sailing on the *Philadelphia*. And so Eva, along with her mother and father, was offered a second-class berth on the *Titanic*. But Eva's mother, who by everyone's description was an even-keeled woman, was troubled by a premonition she had that something dreadful would happen.

On Sunday morning April 14, the ship received a wireless message from the *SS Caronia*, reporting that icebergs had been spotted just a few miles north of *Titanic's* plotted course. Later that same day, *Titanic* received additional ice warnings. One came from the steamship *Baltic* at 1:40 pm, with reports of "passing icebergs and a large quantity of field ice."[1] This message included specific coordinates marking the location of the ice. Another message was received from the *Californian* and reported ice about 19 miles north of *Titanic's* path. Coordinates were provided as well. The German liner *Amerika* sent a message with reports of seeing two large icebergs. Last, another message came through, again from the *Californian*, stating, "We are stopped and surrounded by ice," to which *Titanic's* radio operator wired back, "Shut up. I am busy!"[2]

As the world would later discover, mankind's largest seagoing vessel struck an iceberg at 11:40 pm on April 14, 1912, while traveling around 24 miles per hour. Seven-year-old Eva, asleep at the time, was told later by her mother that it felt like nothing more than a slight bump. Even so, Eva's mother woke her husband, who, after taking the elevator up to the deck, promptly returned to gather his wife and child. Wrapping his daughter in a thick blanket, the man quickly led his family topside. At this early stage following the collision, there was no panic or perceived danger. Even so, as a precaution, Eva and her mother were loaded into a lifeboat, where they waited in the bone-chilling night air.

Assessing the damage and after receiving reports from down below, Captain Smith confirmed the ship was sinking and gave the order to fill the lifeboats.

That's when panic set in.

The *Titanic* went down in 2 hours and 40 minutes, carrying 1512 souls more than two miles below the frigid waters of the North Atlantic. Eva Hart and her mother survived, but she would never see her father again. The young girl watched the huge vessel tip, submerge, and then break in half before going under completely. The scene would forever be etched in her memory.

On the day *Titanic* sank, a lifeboat drill had been scheduled, but for some unknown reason, Captain Smith had canceled the drill. There were other wireless messages and iceberg warnings from additional ships in the area as well. Some were acknowledged, while others were not.

Many safety measures for cruise ships have been enacted since the sinking of the *Titanic*, including evacuation procedures and regulations not in existence prior to this epic event. Sadly, so many perished for those lessons to be learned.

Messages. Warnings. Tragedy.

Like those iceberg warnings of April 1912, Bible prophecies alert us regarding the end times. They warn of approaching danger and give us clues on how to avoid catastrophe. When heeded, they save lives. When ignored, disaster is inevitable. We have seen some of the similarities between Noah's day and the final days of planet earth. We've also observed our own generation's resemblance to these two. Seeing these parallel signs doesn't mean we're about to be raptured any more than spotting an iceberg means a ship is going to sink.

But it does mean we're in the right waters.

And this we do know. There are icebergs all around us. While we may not agree on the specifics, I believe, as do most biblical scholars and prophecy experts, that humanity is on a collision course with God's coming judgment and soon return of His Son, Jesus Christ. We are racing full speed ahead into the night, toward a rendezvous with global catastrophe. Numerous compelling moral, cultural, geopolitical, and biblical evidences indicate we may very well be close to the end times described in Scripture. Some of these signs and clues may sound as unlikely and improbable as a block of ice capsizing an unsinkable ship. There are those who say the chances these prophetic events will really happen are so miniscule as to be thought ridiculous. As absurd as an Ark saving a family and some animals from a worldwide flood. But for the discerning person, there is a growing sense that the world we're on is nearing the conclusion of its journey. And you don't need a premonition to figure that out.

As we observe humanity through the interpretive grid of Scripture, what we see is a generation much like the one in Noah's day. Like Noah's, ours is a world populated by billions uninterested and unconcerned about a prophesied coming judgment. In fact, most today don't even believe there was ever a *first* judgment. To them, the story of Noah, the Ark, the Flood, and the obliteration of humanity is pure fiction. A great idea for a movie, but not real-life historical stuff. They don't believe, as Christians do, that there is a 100 percent chance of rain in the forecast. They don't believe this because, in their eyes, there isn't even a cloud in the sky. There is nothing in their minds or on their radar indicating the world is coming to an end. Nothing convincing them that demons will be released to torment mankind. No impending signs that earthquakes, war, and famine will ravage the earth anytime soon. No one-world government or mythical Antichrist villain. And especially no empirical evidence that a crucified Galilean rabbi from 2000 years ago is returning to earth a second time.

To them it's all sci-fi, apocalyptic fantasy—*Resident Evil, Day After Tomorrow, Book of Eli* stuff. And while it may make for a great campfire story, that's really all it is. This generation doesn't consider themselves to be godless because there's no God anyway. And if He did exist, He would never be so judgmental as to destroy the earth and its inhabitants. They don't see violence as being out of control or epidemic. Abortion is not brutal murder to them.

Besides, there are plenty of good people in the world to counterbalance those who *do* break the law. There is no sexual problem either, especially no mainstream sexual "perversions." And they're offended that there are some who judge and condemn "good people" just because they were born with a different sexual orientation or because they sleep with their girlfriend. And why should anyone care, anyway? I mean, it's still a free country, right? They see Christian views on sexuality as repressive and Victorian. And unrealistic. In their minds, the whole end-times scenario is simply another scare tactic meant to sell a few books and pad box-office revenues. And maybe frighten a few weak-minded people toward the faith.

Providing you happen to actually believe in all this end-times super-stition, you're labeled "not-so-intelligent" and "unscientific." Maybe a wee bit kooky too. You may be a nice person, but your street cred drops dramatically when you start talking about another planet-wide judgment on its way. Besides, God's supposed to love everybody. So just keep your views to yourself and people won't think you've gone off the deep end.

Feel like Noah yet?

Source Code

As previously stated, much about future prophetic events is as of yet unclear. That's why what appear to be signs of the approaching end times are more like gathering storm clouds than actual calendar dates. We may not yet be experiencing those birth pangs Jesus spoke of in Matthew 24, but it's becoming pretty obvious that we are "great with child." As followers of Jesus, our core beliefs about the future come not from opinion or speculation, but from the Word of God. We draw our information, and our confidence, from the truth God supernaturally recorded for us.[3] And the veracity and reliability of the Bible is insepa-rably linked to the trustworthiness of God Himself. So to dismiss the one is to discount the other. For believers, the simple and plain prom-ises of Jesus are enough:

"I go to prepare a place for you. If I go…I will come again" (John 14:2-3).

"I am coming quickly" (Revelation 22:20).

And therein lies our hope, not as in "I wish for," but rather, "I confidently expect."[4] Scripture says all these end-times events "*must* take place" (Revelation 4:1). And since Scripture and Jesus have a 100 percent accuracy record so far when it comes to fulfilled prophecy, they remain a safe bet for the future.

But for billions of people, it's just not reality. They're not getting it because God says they have previously suppressed the truth about Him. They aren't looking for something to happen in the *future*, because they're way too busy enjoying (or stressing out about) the *now*. As a result, they are totally unprepared for what's coming. For them, life is the "same ol' same ol'."

Consumed by self and self-pleasure, these last-days mockers ridicule the very idea of Jesus' return.[5] Their twofold motivation and rationale (besides portraying Christians as foolish and simpleminded) is that "the universe doesn't work like that," and that "there is no God who flooded the earth, so there can't be one that destroys it in the future."[6] This futile attempt at logic is based on taking the observable laws of science and retroactively applying them to ancient civilizations. This presupposes, of course, that there is no God, and if there were, He certainly doesn't punch through the time/space barrier, suspending the laws of nature and interfering in the affairs of men. And why do they believe this? Because after suppressing the evident truth about God, they became "darkened in their understanding, excluded from the life of God because of the ignorance that is in them, because of the hardness of their heart."[7] By necessity, they must come up with an alternate explanation of the universe and why God's Word *can't* be true (or at least why they hope it's not). It's a classic and ultimate case of denial, so much so that they cannot even conceive of God's Word being true, especially regarding the end times. And their denial is deliberate.[8] It's not that they're stupid. Just foolish.[9]

But what is indisputable to both believers and unbelievers is that world boundaries are dissolving and our planet is rapidly becoming one big society. Globalization is merging humanity, giving us communication and a commonality mankind hasn't experienced since the Tower of Babel.[10] Like the *Titanic*, we have set sail, and we *are* going somewhere. But no meteorologist can, with pinpoint accuracy, forecast the coming global storm. Doppler radar won't pick up this prophetic weather event. As with attempting to predict a tornado, we can only know when the *conditions* are right. Dark skies, wall clouds, swirling debris, and large hail indicate a tornado is near. And if the air becomes still and you hear what sounds like a freight train, you can be pretty sure a tornado is imminent, and you should take cover immediately. Similarly, Bible prophecy lets us know the signs that warn of coming events.

Moral, spiritual, and economic conditions on earth will likely become increasingly worse leading up to the rapture. Following this event, a different phase of God's justice will begin, as "sowing and reaping" will give way to another kind of wrath—the apocalyptic kind.

And while we cannot speculate with specificity, of this we are certain—Jesus Christ *is* returning to this planet.[11] Just like He said He would. His triumphant return will include a galloping army of the redeemed, led into battle by their conquering King. These warriors include both angels and believers. In Revelation 19:11-16, John describes his prophetic vision of this event. As he does, we see that the Jesus who appears at the end of the Tribulation is very different from the One we're accustomed to. This Christ, having been resurrected, ascended, and glorified, has been seated at the right hand of the Father since His departure from the earth in AD 30. He's been in heaven, but He hasn't been idle. Instead, He's been occupied with His role as Ruler, Mediator, Intercessor, and Homebuilder.[12] So far He has spent about 2000 years preparing a place especially for His bride, the church. His love for the church is a romance unparalleled and unequaled on earth. During the Tribulation, those believers who were taken up in the rapture will have already settled into their new heavenly home, celebrated the marriage supper of the Lamb, and received their rewards from Jesus Himself.[13]

But now the hour of judgment has come. It's an unbreakable

appointment Christ has with humanity. The second coming of Jesus Christ is more certain than even death itself. Mankind has a rendezvous with retribution. But this judgment is not simply an explosion of anger or the outburst of a hot-tempered deity. Instead, it is the execution of justice upon the wicked by a Righteous King.

The Bible says Satan, his Antichrist, and his second-in-charge, the False Prophet, will gather the armies of planet earth in a place called Armageddon.[14] Located just south of Jesus' hometown of Nazareth, Armageddon (or the Jezreel Valley) will be the site for this epic final battle.[15] This war is actually the last phase of a series of battle campaigns that will take place during the final days of the Tribulation.[16]

The exact spot where Jesus will touch down on earth is the Mount of Olives.[17] This is significant for at least two reasons: (1) It's the same spot from which He ascended into heaven (Acts 1:6-12), and (2) it's the same location where He had told His disciples about end-times events (Matthew 24).[18] The Bible tells us that when He returns, His foot will touch the Mount of Olives, splitting it east to west, creating a large valley through which surviving Jews may flee to safety. Interestingly, seismologists have documented faults in the earth's crust in this region, and they say that conditions are such that a major quake could be expected at any time.[19]

Jesus will burst through the sky, riding not a humble donkey this time, but a white warhorse. "His name is called The Word of God,"[20] the visible revelation of the invisible God.[21] Jesus had warned future generations about false Christs, as if to say, "Don't be fooled by people pretending to be the Christ. Trust Me. When I return, I *guarantee* you'll know it's Me." When Jesus shows up, it will be a personal appearance, and every eye will see Him.[22] He will come not as a tender infant, but a triumphant warrior. The war He will wage is righteous, and the sentence He will execute is predicated upon His holiness and just character.[23] The Judge of all the earth has commanded it.[24]

He is coming to conquer. And to kill.

His eyes are described as "a flame of fire" and upon His head will be many regal crowns,[25] which have long since replaced the crown of thorns He wore at His crucifixion. His suffering has passed. His reigning has begun. John also sees a "name" written upon Him which no one knows except Himself. This mysterious name is perhaps one given to Him by the Father, and is something only the Godhead understands. There is another name, however, that John, the heavenly army, and every earthly inhabitant can understand. This name is written on His robe and on His thigh (perhaps in the form of a banner)—

"KING OF KINGS, AND LORD OF LORDS."[26]

This title proclaims Jesus' absolute sovereignty over all things, and announces His right to judge, make war, and overcome His enemies. The edge of His robe is dipped in blood, possibly symbolic of past victories, but assuredly foreshadowing His victory at Armageddon.

Accompanying Jesus in this climactic battle will be the redeemed from the ages, along with an angelic host.[27] Robed in righteousness, untold millions, including those raptured prior to the beginning of the Tribulation, will follow Him, also mounted on white horses. Jesus is also called "Faithful and True."[28] He had promised to come and receive His bride, and He did at the rapture.[29] He had promised to return to this world, and now He is making good on that promise as well.[30] Jesus never breaks a promise; He fulfills every word He speaks.[31] Descending from the clouds, Jesus will appear to be the only one armed in this climactic campaign. But His weapon is enough. He is armed with the Word, proceeding from his mouth, portrayed as a "sharp sword."[32] Earth's armies will fall before Him by the utterance from His mouth. We don't know what He will say, but it will likely be a pronunciation of judgment.

It will be no contest.

To describe this judgment, John uses the imagery of a winemaker crushing grapes under his feet, spewing out juices that fill up the winepress. Only here, it's the "fierce wrath of God" crushing the wicked.[33] It's more brutal than *Braveheart* and more bloody than Omaha Beach as untold millions are annihilated by the powerful, penetrating Word of God. This judgment will spill an unimaginable amount of blood, which we are told will flow for nearly 200 miles![34]

The mere thought of God's wrath should evoke a holy reverence within us. It not only reminds us that He is just and punishes the wicked, but also cautions us against painting mental caricatures of Him, accentuating His love over His holiness and vice versa.[35] It's difficult to know what we'll be feeling as we follow our King into battle. In our humanity, we may imagine recoiling or even being repulsed at such a massive slaughter of humanity. Surely Noah felt the same way. Perhaps he heard the horrifying sounds of people drowning outside the Ark while the rain descended and the floodwaters rose. He may have momentarily wondered if God's judgment was too harsh. Later, when he stepped off the Ark and realized his family of eight were the only humans still walking the earth, the reality of God's wrath must have lingered strong in his memory.

Likewise, when we consider the future bloodbath at Armageddon, we may wonder if there's the option of staying at home up in heaven while everyone else goes to war. Maybe just let those Christians who are the "soldier types" join Jesus on this mission. But it should comfort us to know that by this time, Christians will have been glorified in Christ, and our salvation will be complete.[36] We will already have been transformed and given new bodies. We will no longer suffer any of the limitations of our old physical bodies, including sickness and temptation. Instead, we will possess a resurrection body like Christ's, not restricted by time and space.[37]

But beyond this physical transformation, we will also be changed in spirit as well. Not only will our sin nature finally be eradicated, but we will be "like Him" as the process of being conformed to His image (begun at salvation) will now be complete.[38] We will possess the mind of Christ in our glorified state, which means we will understand all things from His perspective. This includes the ability to correctly balance and manage not only the terrible wrath of God, but also the indescribable joy of heaven. Until we get to heaven, we cannot fully appreciate either the love *or* wrath of God. But riding behind our Lord on that day, it will all make sense. And there will be no fear—only a triumphant celebration of the victory won by our glorious Savior.

But for those who remain down here on earth, a very different experience awaits. This will be the final judgment upon earth, and the bloodiest in all human history. The Bible says the kings of the earth will be summoned together to the Jezreel Valley by three demonic spirits who perform miraculous signs, inviting them to come.[39] The armies of the whole world will be persuaded to gather here for one purpose— to "wage war against the Lamb." But "the Lamb will overcome them, because He is the Lord of lords and King of kings," and those who are with Him are the "called and chosen and faithful."[40]

Once again, God will destroy those who reject and ignore Him, corrupting themselves with self-worship and a love affair with sin and sensuality. Rainbows will be replaced with retributive justice. Those who loved darkness rather than the light will face judgment that descends from the sky.[41] Earth's mockery of the Son will come to an end. The mouths of skeptics will be forever shut. The only mouths that will be open are those of birds who are summoned by an angel ahead of time to feast on the corpses of kings, commanders, and soldiers.[42] These famished fowls will gorge themselves on the dead bodies of those who defied Him who made the heavens and the earth. Seven years before this, the saints assembled in heaven celebrated "the marriage supper of the Lamb."[43] This post-Armageddon feast is called "the great supper of God."[44] One supper celebrates grace, the other judgment. And like the earlier recipients of Tribulation wrath, those who die in this final battle will "deserve it."[45]

The words of God's gospel-proclaiming angel will ring with chilling clarity: "Fear God, and give Him glory, because the hour of His judgment has come."[46]

That's what will happen in the second global storm.

As happened with the generations leading up to the Flood, God's wrath has been gathering for thousands of years. Part of His judgment through the ages has been to allow man to follow his own choices and for his sin to take its natural cause-and-effect route. Mankind has sown the wind, but will reap the whirlwind.[47] Having become drunk with themselves, people will get more than they bargained for, having expelled God from their lives. As a result, the coming fierce wrath of God will be a fermented and potent drink.[48]

The age of grace in which we live is coming to an abrupt close, and what follows will be a mind-bending, catastrophic conclusion to civilization as we know it.

But until that time, there's something Jesus wants you to do.

The Open Door

The Spirit and the bride say, "Come."

REVELATION 22:17

On December 7, 1941, millions of Americans sat in their living rooms staring at radios, straining to hear reports of what had happened at an obscure naval base on a remote chain of islands called *Hawaii*. The following day, President Franklin Roosevelt, in what is arguably the most memorable speech of his four terms as president, addressed Congress, asking for a declaration of war. At the speech's conclusion, he was met with thunderous applause and a unanimous affirmation.

The next four years would be a test of America's spirit and resolve as an entire nation sacrificed for the war effort. Families did without usual amounts of groceries as ration stamps were distributed, limiting the allowance for such things as meat, sugar, butter, vegetables, and fruit. Instead, Americans grew their own "Victory Gardens" at home. Gasoline was in short supply. You could hardly find a candy bar. Boy Scouts held paper drives while other kids collected rubber, clothing, aluminum—anything that could be used to help the cause. Some churches even melted down their bells for metal. Women became the backbone of the American workforce, laboring at factories and assembling airplanes, tanks, warships, rifles, and ammunition.

And of course, there were the soldiers and sailors. Men couldn't enlist fast enough, as recruitment offices were jammed with our nation's young men, eager to fight for their country. Thousands of teenage boys, like my dad, exaggerated their age for the privilege of joining the military. This conflict, which threatened the future of civilization itself, guaranteed that hardly a soul would be left unaffected. Some worked. Others fought. Everybody prayed.

In a time of war or national crisis or disaster, every area of life is impacted. And everyone pitches in. Like when a hurricane or tornado hits, thousands instinctively rally to help victims. That's just what we do. It seems right. People somehow automatically know it's time to help. The wisest man who ever lived wrote, "There is an appointed time for everything. And there is a time for every event under heaven."[1]

We as Christians now find ourselves in a unique era of human history. At no other time since the first coming of Christ has end-times prophecy seemed so feasible. The events outlined in Scripture concerning the last days are no longer relegated to futuristic fantasies or the religious rants of wannabe prophets scurrying about the periphery of mainstream Christianity. The prototypical street-corner doomsday prophet wearing a "THE END IS NEAR" sandwich sign may still seem a bit oddball, but his message isn't quite as absurd as it once seemed. Not since the early church first received the New Testament letters has there been such a spirit of expectancy among students of the Bible and prophecy.

Before World War II, it was hard to imagine how some of Revelation's prophecies could take place. Not anymore. So much has changed since then. Exponential advancements in technology. The concerted move toward a unified government in Europe. The increasing development toward a global economy. Volatile relationships between opposing nations. And perhaps most of all, the regathering of the Jewish people to Israel in 1948, making much of prophecy seem plausible for the first time since AD 70![2] Prophecy expert Dr. Mark Hitchcock writes, "Almost all of the key events of the end times hinge on the existence of the nation of Israel," calling their return to the land a "supersign" of the end times. Hitchcock adds, "Since the Tribulation officially begins with the Antichrist making a seven-year treaty with Israel (Daniel 9:27)...obviously for this to happen, Israel must exist. The Jews must be back in their land."[3] This is now happening. Today there are more Jews living in Israel than anywhere else on earth, second only to the United States.

Further, as we survey Scripture, we see there are no more prophe-cies that need to be fulfilled in order for the rapture to occur. Nothing needed to trigger this coming prophetic event. It's the next red-letter date on God's prophetic calendar. He will simply give the order, and Jesus will shout as He descends from heaven.[4] The archangel (Michael) will follow with a shout of his own. Then the "trumpet of God" will sound. Trumpets are used by God to announce judgment,[5] but this is a trumpet of celebration, summoning Jesus' bride to the wedding feast. Christians in the grave will rise, their bodies reunited with their spirits coming from heaven. Christians alive at this time will be "caught up" (raptured) together with them to "meet the Lord in the air."[6] At the same time, our bodies will be transformed and glorified.[7] All this will happen "in the twinkling of an eye."[8] That's God's way of saying it will happen very fast, as in *instantly*. This explains why the rapture is often described or portrayed as believers "disappearing."

No planes, trains, or automobiles will be needed for this trip. It will be a supernatural, lightning-speed transport to meet Jesus in the sky.

Another reason we know the rapture is the next major biblical pro-phetic event to happen is because the early church treated this event as *imminent*. In other words, they believed it could happen at any moment. Some who are critical of this view say it is a relatively recent belief, stemming from the teachings of a nineteenth-century evange-list. However, there are way too many scriptures indicating otherwise.[9] The first-century church looked for Christ to come back at any time!

Paul wrote of "*looking* for the blessed hope and the appearing of the glory of our great God and Savior, Christ Jesus."[10] The author of Hebrews said, "So Christ also, having been offered once to bear the sins of many, will appear a second time for salvation without reference to sin, to those who *eagerly await* Him."[11]

Why would you be "looking for" and "eagerly await" something unless you expected it to happen at any time? The early Christians lived with a sense of anticipation. They believed their Savior could return at any time to rescue them from the coming wrath. There is no other way to explain this widespread and pervasive attitude of expectancy in the early church—unless, of course, Scripture itself is wrong and they were mistaken. The imminent expectancy of the rapture is why it's called the "blessed hope" in Titus 2:13. This spirit of expectancy does something to Christians, changing the way they relate to God, one another, the church, and the world.

In the "Bling" of an Eye

While in college, I was part of a large Christian student organization. One day a speaker came to our group and spoke on this topic of the rapture, emphasizing that it could occur at any time. Following the meeting, one girl promptly went back to her sorority and began giving away all her jewelry (and those sorority girls had a lot of bling!). She did this because she took the speaker's words literally, expecting Jesus to come back at any time. But what my friend failed to realize is that having this expectation didn't require her to give away all her earthly possessions. Besides, what did her actions say about what she thought of her sorority sisters?! Once this girl realized her misapplication of Scripture, she began recollecting her jewelry from her friends. I still laugh when I think of her making the rounds at her sorority house, explaining why she needed her necklaces and earrings back. "Um, so like Jesus might not come back this week after all, and I kinda need those earrings for a party this Friday, soooooo...if you don't mind...thank you."

So if we're not supposed to give all our stuff away or gather commune-style on some local mountain and wait for Jesus, what *should* we do? Believing that Christ's return for His bride is imminent, by definition, means *we don't know* when it will happen. It could happen before you finish this book. Or it could happen in a year, or 10 or 50 years from now. No one knows. Only God possesses that information.

But while the New Testament clearly teaches an imminent rapture, it is also filled with plenty of truth and teaching to keep us occupied in the meantime. Knowing that Christ will snatch away His bride before the coming wrath is unleashed should motivate us to be *ready*. Over the years I've performed some 75 weddings. One of the joys of being a minister is playing a part in joining two lives together. And I've had some awesome experiences in that role. But though both bride and groom eagerly await that day, the bride usually spends that time preparing *herself.* The groom, however, stays busy getting the house or apartment cleaned and ready, and managing the finances or logistics of their future life together. He's also praying the rapture doesn't happen before the wedding night!

When it comes to the rapture, Christ wants His bride to be ready for Him. Like a bride before her wedding day, Jesus wants us to be pure.[12] The apostle John says the reason for this is so that "when He appears, we may have confidence and not shrink away from Him in shame at His coming."[13] If a man asked his fiancée not to sleep around during their engagement, no one would think he is a control freak or treating his soon-to-be wife unfairly. He just loves her, and they have promised themselves exclusively to one another. In the same way, Jesus' commands regarding preparation and purity flow out of a heart of love for His bride. He just wants us to live worthy lives. That's why He asks us to remain close to Him, practice righteousness, and abide in His love.[14]

Another thing God wants us to do is to continue living like we normally would as followers of Christ. If we knew Jesus was returning this Thursday at 6:31 pm, we would probably tell everyone we knew— then, leading up to the moment, maybe pray, sing some songs, celebrate, and wait. It would be like a really intense tailgate party (we may even give away some of our jewelry). But since we don't know the date and time of the rapture, we are to just keep on doing what we're supposed to do. Martin Luther, the great reformer, summed up this sentiment well by writing, "Even if I knew that tomorrow the world would go to pieces, I would still plant my apple tree." Just being obedient in what we should do today is what God wants. Put another way, "Look for Christ, but keep on living."

At the same time, we also should be careful not to act like He will *never* return. God wants us to be trustworthy stewards of what we've been given. Speaking of His return, Jesus told His disciples a parable about servants investing what their master had entrusted to them. The servants who invested wisely were rewarded, while the one who did nothing with his master's resources was chastised and punished.[15] Jesus had earlier warned these servants to "be on the alert…for you do not know the day nor the hour."[16] This highlights not only our need to be faithful with what we've been given, but also to live with a sense of urgency about our lives.

There is plenty to do while waiting expectantly for Jesus to return. The important stuff. The daily stuff. Family. Work. School. Church. Life stuff. Good stuff. God stuff. Noah didn't know the exact day the Flood would come, though he had a pretty good idea it wouldn't happen until he finished the Ark. But even then he didn't know the precise day. He also was aware of Methuselah's prophecy-name, but had no idea when the old man would die or how long after his death "it" would come. So what was he to do? Sit around staring at the sky? Philosophize about the future and judgment? Rant about evil? Negative. Noah had work to do. He had a mission. He understood God had given him a very special task, and in order to accomplish it, he would have to get busy and *stay* busy, focusing on the things that really matter. He simply worked hard and waited to hear God's voice.[17]

Noah knew *who* he was, *why* he was here, and *where* he was going in life. Too many Christians coast along in their lives without any direction. They get up. Go to school or work. Come home. And repeat the same monotony day after day. They fill their time with friends, hobbies, entertainment, or family. Once or twice a week they might focus on God at church or some Christian activity, but these are often mere punctuation marks in their lives, not the crux of who they are. Most believers are content just knowing their ticket on the Ark has been purchased by Jesus. They take great comfort from having a reserved seat on the Rapture Express, and that there's a home in heaven with their name on the mailbox. But eternal life is much more than what lies ahead. It's also about the *now*. Understanding who you are, how you've been gifted, and what you have to offer the body of Christ and the world is necessary if you're going to make your life count here on earth. Live like a person with purpose!

God probably won't ask you to build a giant floating zoo. But He *is* asking you to do *something* for Him. He made you unique and special. And there are things you can do that no one else can. You have a unique "fragrance," a life fingerprint, a memorable mark to leave on the world.[18] And though your mission may not involve a hammer and saw, it will involve *building* something. For most, it begins with family, and then fans outward from there. God wants you to build a life that invites others to the salvation He offers. Through your words, example, and relationships, your life represents hope to those who need refuge from the coming tempest of judgment. Some people may not like the life you're building. Your work of faith may draw more jeers than cheers. Your belief in biblical morality or the person and work of Christ may even elicit hate from some.

They may call you names.

You may be thought a bigot or narrow-minded fundamentalist. People may say you're crazy. That you believe in a myth. That you're mean for saying Jesus is the only way to heaven. That you're dumb and unscientific for trusting in the Bible. But we who are Christians must have a thick skin regarding such things. At the same time, we have to maintain a tender heart.

A tender heart.

That's not a phrase you hear a lot when talking about the end of the world. It's not typically one of the main points in a sermon on the last days, either. Simply mention God's judgment in the Flood, the current state of our world, or the coming Tribulation, and the last thing people will say about you is that you have a tender heart. As we've seen, Christians and their beliefs will become more and more vilified and demonized in the last days. Our views and values will become increasingly unpopular and even outlawed, socially speaking. But don't be surprised. Jesus said these things would happen.[19] Don't place unrealistic expectations on those who do not know Christ. Don't expect them to "get it." They won't, and according to Jesus and Paul, they *can't* without divine help.[20]

And that's another reason you need a tender heart. This book began with a look at the broken heart of God over His creation. It grieved His Spirit when He saw how depraved mankind had become. So corrupted was humanity that God lamented its very creation. And because of His righteous character, He had to administer judgment and recompense to man the wages of his sin. Yet even then He offered hope. Even then He was patient. And there is no patience like the patience of God. No willingness to endure like His. As long as there was breath in Methuselah's lungs, there was hope. As long as Noah swung a hammer, salvation was possible. As long as the Ark door remained open, deliverance from judgment was an option. *That's* the tender heart of our compassionate God.

And that's the same heart you and I must have as well. As we look at our generation, much like Noah did at his, we see a world of people—lost, blind, sensual, violent, godless, and self-serving. Some are vile and immoral and without faith, while others are religious and decent. However, frequently it is the "good" people who are the hardest to convince of their need for a Savior. But no matter how an individual ends up living their life without God, no sin or sins are so great that Jesus can't forgive.[21] With Jesus Christ, *all* sin is washed away for the one who trusts in Him. Idolaters? Covered. Homosexuals? Declared righteous. Drunkards? Given a fresh start. Adulterers? Cleansed. Fornicators? Forgiven. Self-righteous right-wing conservatives? Transformed. Observant church members? Made new.

Earlier this year, I spoke in Colchester, England. With a history dating back to the first century, Colchester is widely considered Britain's oldest town. While touring the area with a local pastor, we visited Roman ruins, including the still-standing Roman wall that once protected the town. We also stood on the remains of what is believed to be the first Christian church in England, dating back to the fourth century. But there was one site that intrigued me even more than these. It's an obscure little building that is nearly invisible from the small side street where it's located. Back in 1850, it was a tiny Primitive Methodist chapel. On Sunday, January 6 of that year, a snowstorm blanketed Colchester. Fifteen-year-old Charles Spurgeon had set out from home that morning to attend a church in Tollesbury, some 12 miles away, where his father had been appointed a pastor. But the snowstorm cut his travels short and Charles went looking for a local place of worship. Due to the cold and snow, he ended up turning down a side street and entered the tiny chapel.

With only about a dozen people in attendance that snowy morning, young Spurgeon stood out as a visitor. The small congregation sang so loud it gave him a headache, but he didn't care. He was just glad to be out of the cold. The regular minister was absent that day, and in his place was an uneducated speaker. A thin man. Spurgeon later recalled thinking he was a shoemaker or tailor. The man's sermon was simple. "Look unto me, and be ye saved, all the ends of the earth: for I am God, and there is none else." [22] So unrefined was this man that he didn't even pronounce the words correctly. However, so hungry for salvation was Spurgeon that it didn't matter. The guest preacher continued:

> Look unto Me; I am sweatin' great drops of blood. Look unto Me; I am hangin' on the cross. Look unto Me; I am dead and buried. Look unto Me; I rise again. Look unto Me; I ascend to Heaven. Look unto Me; I am sittin' at the Father's right hand. O poor sinner, look unto Me! Look unto Me! [23]

Then the preacher stared out into the small crowd, and fixing his eyes on the teenage boy, he said, "Young man, you look very miserable, and you always will be miserable—miserable in life, and miserable in death—if you don't obey my text; but if you now obey, this moment, you will be saved." Then, lifting up his hands, he shouted, "Young man, look to Jesus Christ. Look! Look! Look! You have nothin' to do but to look and live!"

Spurgeon later said at once he understood the way of salvation. Schooled by an uneducated man, he looked to Christ and was saved. He went on to become the greatest preacher in the English language, with some estimating he may have spoken to as many as ten million people in his lifetime. Even today he is still one of the most widely read preachers in history, with many of his books still in print worldwide.

God's call to salvation is simple. To anyone who needs deliverance from sin, He simply says, "Come." Look to Him and be saved.

The gospel of Jesus Christ is good news for sinners, and everyone who calls on the name of the Lord will be saved. [24] It is not yet too late. People can still be rescued. It has not yet begun to "rain," and you don't want your family, friends, and others to miss this boat. Jesus is the Door to the Ark and the Ark itself! And you are God's mouthpiece to

your generation.[25] Some may view this truth about impending judgment as a mere scare tactic designed to elicit a response. This would
be a tragic self-deception, and no doubt one that the people in Noah's
day experienced. Someone once defined hell as "truth seen too late."
And for many, even a flood won't convince them. But it doesn't have
to be this way.

Prophecy about the end times is a sobering alarm, alerting mankind
to the coming judgment. God's provision is offered, and the way of
escape is available. There is still opportunity and great hope! The
turning of these pages has been, as it were, the sound of hammers
pounding, echoing prophetic truth concerning where we are in history.
And every believer heeding these words from Scripture carries the spirit
of Noah and the message of Jesus to their generation.

I urge you to not be like those Christians whose lack of biblical
knowledge and understanding makes them unaware of prophecy and
the blessed hope they have in Jesus. Don't be like the many church
members who can neither articulate a general template for the end
times nor recognize any sign pointing to the latter days. So caught up
in this life and their own pursuits, such things are not a priority for
them. This is unfortunate. For believers, the approaching hoofbeats of
God's judgment aren't some apocalyptic horror story. It's a call to get
ready. To remain pure. To live with purpose. And to offer the gospel
with your life and mouth.

Noah's generation was not left without a witness. God wove for
mankind a testimonial tapestry of evidence. He gave them creation and
consciences. He sent messengers. He even built a gargantuan wooden
object lesson. And for 120 years, He waited.

Today we have even more specific revelation about God than Noah's
world had. We know about past judgments and the future coming of
Jesus. We know about the completion of Scripture and the fulfillment
of latter-day prophecies. If those destroyed in the Flood were held
accountable having only limited knowledge, what will the condemnation of today's generation be like in light of all that's been revealed
by God?[26]

The door of the Ark was open for a very long time, symbolizing hope and salvation. And today, God is holding open the door. Right now.[27] Jesus is sending a bloodstained invitation to our generation. He longs to spare unbelievers from the wrath to come. He is pleading for them to see not only their need and His coming judgment, but more than anything, His great love for them.[28] He wants to make them whole.[29] To make them a part of His bride.

This ancient tale of a big boat has a lot more to do with our lives than we might expect. The Ark is rising from the waters of history as a last-days reminder that God is patient and stands ready to deliver people from the coming global storm.

In the meantime, I hear hammers pounding.

Notes

Introduction

1. The Chinese legend speaks of a man named *Fuhi*, who, with his wife and three sons, survives a great flood and afterward begins repopulating the earth as the single surviving family. The Hawaiian account speaks of a man called *Nu-u*, who built a massive canoe, put a house on it, and packed it with animals. Then water covered the earth and only Nu-u and his family were saved.

2. 2 Peter 3:5-6.

3. Matthew 24:1-3,36-39.

4. Matthew 24:35.

5. For more on the earth's population before the Flood, see endnote 7 in chapter 1.

Chapter 1—The Days of Noah

1. Ephesians 4:30.

2. Isaiah 63:10; Matthew 23:37; Ephesians 4:30.

3. Psalm 8:3-6.

4. Genesis 1:28.

5. Genesis 2:18,23-25.

6. Genesis 6:1.

7. See http://bible-truth.org/GEN6.HTM; http://www.ldolphin.org/pickett.html.

8. Genesis 1:28.

9. Romans 3:23.

10. Jeremiah 17:9 (NKJV).

11. Genesis 19:1-29. The devastation of the twin cities of Sodom and Gomorrah occurred roughly 500 years after the Flood, and after humanity had rebooted through Noah. Evidently man's wickedness quickly deteriorated again on an international scale, resulting in a catastrophic divine judgment. The Bible says the men of Sodom craved homosexual relations so intensely that even after being struck blind by God's angels they "wearied themselves" trying to get into Lot's house to molest the angels (who had taken the form of men). Early that next morning, Scripture records, "The LORD rained on Sodom and Gomorrah brimstone and fire from the LORD out of heaven" (Genesis 19:24), destroying the cities, their inhabitants, and everything that grew on the ground.

12. *The Purge*, Universal Pictures, 2013.

13. Romans 1:32.

14. Genesis 6:2.

15. Genesis 4:26.

16. Luke 3:23-38.

17. Genesis 6:3-4.

18. This view sees these "beautiful women" as being a part of the ungodly lineage of Cain. Thus they married outside their godly heritage and corrupted the morals of Seth's godly line, producing the end result of Genesis 6:5 (moral decline, continual sin, etc.).

19. Job 1:6; 2:1; 38:7; Daniel 3:25.

20. 2 Peter 2:4-5; see also Jude 6.

21. Isaiah 14:12-15; Ezekiel 28:12-19.

22. Matthew 25:41; Luke 12:48; 1 Corinthians 6:3; Hebrews 2:14-16; 2 Peter 2:4; Revelation 20:10.

    From these verses we understand several truths:

    • Salvation is not offered to fallen angels, and therefore they cannot be saved.
    • God has no intention of saving angels.
    • Angels are held to a higher standard because of their high position.
    • Christians will have a part in judging angels.
    • The devil will be tormented day and night forever.
    • Hell was created originally and specifically for the devil and his fallen angels.

23. Genesis 1:26.

24. Isaiah 14:14.

25. Because of the Flood, God effectively preserved a godly remnant of humanity unstained by satanic influence to the degree Noah's contemporaries were. It was through Noah's lineage that the Messiah eventually came.

26. Matthew 22:30. In this passage, Jesus does not distinguish between good angels and bad ones (demons). Again, after Satan's heavenly rebellion, all angelic beings were "sealed" in their postre-bellion state, thus preventing bad angels from being redeemed and good angels from becoming bad. If Jesus was referring solely to good angels in this verse, then He was simply stating that they (in their godly state) were not capable of marital relationships (as well as sexual relationships) with mortals. He does not address whether demons could have sexual relations while in human form. Or He could just be talking about marriage in general, without implying any sexual connotation.

27. Genesis 18:1-2,8; 19:1,5.

28. Genesis 19:1-3.

29. Genesis 19:5.

30. Numbers 13:33.

31. Genesis 6:11-12.

32. In Genesis 3:16, God told Eve that sin's effect on women would be an unnatural desire to dominate ("rule over") men. A combination of brutal chauvinism in men and defiant desire to rule in women would make for explosive conflict between the sexes, along with eventual violence. Even so, like today, some in both genders surely permitted themselves to be dominated (sexually, emotionally, and physically) by others.

33. World English Bible.

34. Genesis 3:21.

35. 1 John 2:2.

36. Genesis 4:2.

37. Hebrews 11:4.

38. Genesis 4:4.

39. Genesis 4:5.

40. Genesis 4:7.

41. *Teshuqah* is the same word Moses used in Genesis 3:16, explaining the curse brought to women by Eve's sin. He said her "desire" would be for her husband. This is not a reference to sexual intimacy, but instead refers to a desire to "rule or control," as made clear by the next phrase, "and he shall *rule* over you."

42. Without salvation and the Spirit, we are powerless to obey God's law (Romans 8:6-8). Cain nevertheless could choose to overcome by "doing well" by submitting his will to God (Genesis 4:7). Even unbelievers can relinquish control of their own hearts—especially when God Himself is saying, "You can do this!"

43. John 3:12.

44. John 8:44.

45. Matthew 5:21-22.

Chapter 2—The Last (Righteous) Man on Earth

1. Genesis 6:8.

2. See 2 Corinthians 6:14-18.

3. John 17:16.

4. John 17:11,14-18; Romans 12:2.

5. Matthew 23.

6. Genesis 5:29. The name *Noah* means "rest."

7. The Lamech who descended from Cain introduced the practice of bigamy (having multiple wives). He also had three sons who became pioneers in livestock, music, and metallurgy. After announcing to his wives that he had killed a young man, he boasted that if anyone attempted to punish him for the murder, he would be avenged ten times more than his ancestor, Cain (Genesis 4:23-24). After appealing to God, Cain had been told by the Lord that whoever killed Cain would have vengeance taken out on him sevenfold (Genesis 4:15). This arrogant attitude is sharply contrasted by the other Lamech (Noah's father).

8. Deuteronomy 6:4-9.

9. The phrase "as old as Methuselah" is a standard expression used to describe a very old person. The phrase can be traced back to at least the fourteenth century. An allusion to it is cited circa 1390 in F.J. Furnivall's *Minor Poems*, 1901: "...if a Mon may libben heer As longe as dude Matussale."

10. Genesis 5:24.

11. Hebrews 11:5: "By faith Enoch was taken from this life, so that he did not experience death: 'He could not be found, because God had taken him away.' For before he was taken, he was commended as one who pleased God" (NIV).

12. Jude 14-15.

13. Jude 11. Jude applies Enoch's prophecy to false teachers in the first century and in the end times to those who follow the "way of Cain" and those who rebel against God's truth and authority. Since rampant rebellion was taking place in Enoch's day, he surely applied his announcement to them as well, his prophecy having a contemporary meaning.

14. 2 Kings 2:3,5.

15. Genesis 4:26.

16. At the time of Noah's birth, Methuselah and several generations of his ancestors were still alive, including Enosh (Enoch having been already raptured to heaven). They would all die during Noah's lifetime.

17. 1 Corinthians 1:22-25. Though Jesus and Paul performed signs and miracles, these were meant to be temporary measures until the truth of the gospel began to be proclaimed. As we read the New Testament, we see a gradual dropoff of miracles used to authenticate the Christian message. In their place, Christ's love for the world and gospel truth proclaimed through believers becomes His chosen method. This continues until the end times (Revelation), when God's miracles will be used to bring judgment. People aren't persuaded to belief in Jesus because they see a miracle. Rather, they believe when they see Jesus in Christians and are convinced of their need for Him through the gospel.

18. Genesis 6:13.

19. The same thing occurs in Genesis 3 when the serpent speaks to Eve. She responds to him no differently than she would to anyone else, without even a hint of surprise in her voice. Eve carries on a conversation with the satanically indwelt snake like it was an everyday occurrence. The Lord appears to speak audibly to Adam as well, and the man responds likewise.

20. For example, God told a military general to conquer a city with a marching band of trumpet blowers (Joshua 6:1-5). Another time He directed the prophet Elisha to tell a man to be healed from leprosy by simply washing himself in the Jordan River (2 Kings 5:1-14). When asked about paying a temple tax, Jesus told Peter to cast a hook in the water and take the first fish that bites. He obeyed, and the fish he caught had a coin in its mouth, exactly equal to the amount needed to cover two people in the temple tax (Matthew 17:24-27). God told Isaiah to walk around naked for three years (Isaiah 20:2-3). He commanded Ezekiel to lie on his left side for 390 days while he prophesied, then to do the same thing on his right side for 40 more days (Ezekiel 4:1-8).

21. Genesis 6:14 actually says "gopher wood," which may refer to a cedar or cypress wood, thought to be abundant in the mountains of ancient Armenia and Chaldea. But since we don't know exactly where Noah lived, this is hard to say. It could also be a reference to the method in which the wood was prepared or pieced together.

22. See http://creation.com/the-pitch-for-noahs-ark. As this website states, pitch has not always been made from coal tar and petroleum. For more than 1000 years, European shipbuilders utilized tree resin in sealing and waterproofing their vessels. It is possible that Noah used this method.

23. Genesis 6:13.

24. Genesis 6:17.

25. Genesis 6:19-20.

26. Due to the enormous size of the Ark (1.4 million cubic feet), it's estimated that it could hold 125,000 sheep. There are approximately 18,000 species of animals today (see, for example, http://www.icr.org/article/1105/), and even if that number were doubled in Noah's day, with male and female, that would equal 72,000 animals, leaving plenty of food storage space for both the animals and Noah's family.

27. Numbers 22:28; Jonah 1:17; John 21:5-6.

28. See Isaiah 1:3.

29. Genesis 2:5.

30. Genesis 1:7.

31. Genesis 3:3-4; Romans 3:23; 6:23.

32. Genesis 2:5-6.

33. Genesis 5:32. God spoke to Noah at age 480, 120 years before the Flood. His sons were born when he was 500, so presumably 30 years or so of construction passed before they were old enough to begin helping.

34. Hebrews 11:7.

35. 1 Peter 3:19-20—Christ preached through Noah to his generation.

36. 2 Peter 2:5.

37. 1 Corinthians 1:18-29.

38. See James 2:14-26.

39. Genesis 6:22.

40. Hebrews 11 lists some of the great men and women of faith.

41. Hebrews 11:38.

42. See Philippians 3:20.

43. Genesis 7:2; 8:20.

44. Genesis 7:1,4-5,15-16.

Chapter 3—Deluge

1. This necessary amount of work explains God's command for them to board the vessel seven days prior to the Flood.

2. Moses records the events leading up to the Flood in his characteristc summary writing style:
   - God commands Noah to enter the Ark (Genesis 7:1).
   - Noah obeys the Lord (Genesis 7:1,4,7,9,13,16).
   - Seven days pass (Genesis 7:4,10).
   - God shuts the door of the Ark (Genesis 7:14-16).
   - The Flood comes (Genesis 7:6,10-12,17).

3. 1 Peter 3:20.

4. Romans 2:4-6.

5. Jeremiah 17:9; John 2:24; Romans 3:10-12.

6. See Romans 8:7.

7. See John 10:9.

8. Genesis 7:10-12.

9. Since Moses originally wrote the Pentateuch (the first five books of the Bible) specifically for the people of Israel, he would have likely used a Jewish calendar to communicate dates such as this. If that is true, then the timing of the Flood would roughly correspond to our month of May, about 4362 years ago. These calculations are based on the biblical record and genealogies, and are derived from a literal, grammatical, historical, comprehensive interpretation of Scripture.

10. Angels are well aware of God's activity on the earth, as they are often dispatched to carry out His will. Scripture says that the angelic host rejoices with celebration when one sinner repents (Luke 15:7,10). If angels exhibit great joy when God saves a sinner, what must the mood of heaven have been like when He destroyed billions of them? Were they troubled? Sorrowful like God

had been? Did they mourn the loss of creation and mankind? Or did they tremble in reverential awe at God's holiness and justice?

11. Evidence in the fossil record suggests this event sparked a series of global volcanic eruptions, launching lava, debris, and steam miles up into the sky—see http://www.answersingenesis.org/home/area/tools/flood-waters.asp. Dr. John Morris notes, "Up to 70% of what comes out of volcanoes today is water, often in the form of steam."

12. Today, if our planet's mountains and ocean basins were to be leveled out, there is so much water that the earth's entire surface would be covered 1.7 miles deep in water! (see http://www.answersingenesis.org/articles/nab/really-a-flood-and-ark).

13. Our planet was very different before the Flood, appearing as another world altogether. The temperature, climate, and atmosphere were much more conducive for life and longevity. Noted scientist Henry Morris has written (based on Genesis 1:7) that above the earth existed a "vast blanket of invisible water vapor, translucent to the light of the stars and producing a marvelous greenhouse effect which maintained mild temperatures from pole to pole, thus preventing air-mass circulation and the resultant rainfall (Genesis 2:5). It would certainly have had the further effect of efficiently filtering harmful radiation from space, markedly reducing the rate of somatic mutations in living cells, and, as a consequence, drastically decreasing the rate of aging and death" (Henry Morris, *Scientific Creationism* [San Diego, CA: Master Books, 1984], p. 211).

The magnitude of the global wraparound canopy would explain how the sky could produce 40 days and nights of constant rainfall. This water canopy shielding the earth would also explain why organisms could survive longer in this enhanced oxygen atmosphere. This accounts for why the average pre-Flood life span of specific individuals listed in Genesis was 910 years. This water canopy would also have facilitated the distribution of heat evenly around the planet, also preventing the formation of violent weather. Modern experiments with Hyperbaric Biosphere Chambers attempting to recreate pre-Flood oxygen levels and protection from ultraviolet radiation have resulted in tripling the life spans of some organisms. (http://www.genesispark.com/exhibits/early-earth/hyperbaric).

14. Noah was 480 years old when God spoke to him and 600 when the Flood came 120 years later; Methuselah was 969—see Genesis 5:27.

15. To put it in perspective, it's like being a 70-year-old man (with a life expectancy of 80).

16. According to Genesis 5:20, Methuselah broke his granddad Jared's record of 962, outliving him by 7 years.

17. We know from Genesis 5:25 that Methuselah was 187 when his son Lamech (Noah's father) was born, and that Lamech was 182 when Noah was born. 187+182=369. So Methuselah was 369 years old when Noah was born. Genesis 7:6 states that 600 years after Noah's birth, the Flood came, making Methuselah 969 years old at the time of the Flood, which is also the *exact* year he died. Thus "his death shall bring it."

18. In naming him "his death shall bring it," Methuselah's father perhaps inaugurated his own prophetic ministry. Could this be another reason God took Enoch prematurely to heaven—to spare him from witnessing the devastating fulfillment of his own divine oracle?

19. See Ezekiel 18:32; 33:11; Romans 9:1-3.

20. Genesis 7:17.

21. Matthew 5:44.

22. Numbers 16:31-33.

23. Luke 17:26-27.

24. One may try and argue that Jesus never said anything about Noah, but that His disciples merely "added" that verse. But 2000 years of Scripture, church history, literary criticism, theology, and logic would argue otherwise.

25. A.W. Tozer, *Knowledge of the Holy* (New York: HarperOne, 2009), p. 1.

26. Isaiah 45:5.

27. See Isaiah 40:25.

28. Genesis 1:1,26; Isaiah 40:12-14,21,26.

29. Psalm 19:1-6; Romans 1:18-23; 2:14-16.

30. Psalm 103:19; 115:3; 135:5-6; Daniel 4:35.

31. Isaiah 40:23-25; Revelation 19:16.

32. Philippians 2:10-11; Revelation 20:11-15.

33. See Job 40:3-4.

34. Acts 2:22-23; 4:28-29.

35. Psalm 119:37; 145:7.

36. Ephesians 4:17-20.

37. Ephesians 2:1-3.

38. John 3:36; Romans 5:12; 6:23.

39. See Ezekiel 18:23,32; John 5:40; 1 Timothy 2:4; 2 Peter 3:9.

40. Genesis 7:23.

41. Genesis 7:12,24; 8:4.

42. The search for evidence of the Ark continues with periodic expeditions to the mountains of Ararat. If the biblical account is true, the Ark may still not exist today due to shifts and movements in ice over thousands of years, essentially splintering the ship's wood into indistinguishable pieces. It's also possible Noah and his family dismantled the Ark for firewood.

    God might not allow the Ark to be found for two reasons: (1) He prefers we trust by faith the testimony of His Word and His Son; (2) He knows the inherent religious heart of man would exploit the discovery, commercializing it or turning it (or its parts) into objects of veneration and idolatrous worship.

    If, however, God does allow its remains to be definitively discovered and confirmed, it could be a final last-days evidence of Scripture's veracity, and yet another call for a sinful human race to remember the Flood and repent.

43. Noah spent a total of about 377 days inside the Ark (John F. Walvoord and Roy B. Zuck, eds., *The Bible Knowledge Commentary* (Wheaton, IL: Victor Books, 1983), p. 39.

44. Genesis 7:2-3; 8:20.

45. Genesis 6:18.

46. They are as follows:

    • Reissuing the command to "be fruitful and multiply, and fill the earth" (Genesis 8:17; 9:1).

    • Renewed dominion over the animal kingdom (9:2).

    • Freedom to eat meat from animals, minus the blood (9:3-4). It is possible that one of the heinous offenses practiced by pre-Flood humanity was the consumption of blood (human and animal) as a pagan ritual or symbolic of conquering a neighboring tribe or enemy. God would later devote a section of the Mosaic Law to prohibitions against consuming the blood of animals. Blood represents life, and as such, is sacred to God. Eating the blood represented disrespect for life. It also was a symbol for atonement and sacrifice for sins, so was to be treated with respect (Leviticus 17:1-16; Deuteronomy 12:16,23-25; 1 Samuel 14:32-33; Hebrews 9:12-14; 1 Peter 1:18-19).

- The establishment of capital punishment on those who committed murder. Apparently, in a pre-Flood earth society, there had been few, if any, lawful repercussions for murder. Now there would be a just and fair punishment for wrongly taking the life of those created in the image of God (Genesis 9:6).

- The establishment of a covenant (commonly called the Noahic Covenant), in which God promised to Noah and his sons to never again send a flood to destroy the earth (9:8-11).

- The creation of the rainbow as a visible sign of this covenant (9:12-17). The existence of this multicolored bow was not possible before the Flood. But due to the new infusion of sunlight and post-Flood atmospheric conditions, it now was. It is God's symbol of promise to humanity.

- The human race would begin again through the three sons of Noah. Present in the genetics of these three men were the physical characteristics for the entire human race. Every living person today ultimately traces back to the line of these three (Genesis 9:18-19).

47. Genesis 9:22.

48. Genesis 9:25; see also Exodus 20:5-6, where under the Mosaic Law, God punished sons for the sins of their fathers.

49. Two main interpretations are possible here:

1. Ham looked upon his father's nakedness with great delight, to the point of engaging in some type of sexual act on the unconscious man, either oral or manual stimulation (see Leviticus 18:6-18 and 20:17, where this same author, Moses, addressed the issue of immoral sexual relationships among God's people). Genesis 9:24 says that when Noah awoke from his drunken stupor, he was aware of what "his youngest son had *done to him*." This would lead us to conclude that some sexual act had definitely been performed on him. It is also possible that Ham's son, Canaan, was cursed because (a) he either accompanied his father in the act, or (b) perhaps because he was Ham's favorite. Keep in mind, Noah's sons are never called "righteous" or "blameless" before God, as Noah had been. Though they had, by faith, helped build the Ark, the Bible never says they "walked with God" as their father had. They were sons of a righteous man, but there's no guarantee they were also seekers of God, at least in the way their father was (see Genesis 19:31-36 where this sort of paternal incest also occurred with Lot's daughters, who got their father drunk in order to sleep with him and become pregnant). On the contrary, it's highly probable Noah's sons still carried some of the influence and morality of a pre-Flood culture. At least in this case, Ham certainly exhibited some of that behavior. Contributing to this was the fact that Ham, like his father, had an active sin nature. Every person is pulled toward sin in their own unique way. If this is what happened, apparently Canaan's descendants inherited the sexual morals of their ancestor, Ham, as God sternly warned Israel to avoid the Canaanites' immoral practices (Exodus 23:23-24; Leviticus 18:1-18).

2. Another possibility is that Ham greatly dishonored his father by ridiculing his drunkenness and mocking his uncovered body. This may sound rather silly to us in our day, where respect for parents (or any authority, for that matter) is trivialized. But in Noah's day (and particularly

among his godly genealogy), nakedness was likely still seen as a symbol of shame and sin, a passed-on value from their ancestors in the Garden. Nakedness was also considered shameful in later Hebrew culture, and dishonoring a parent could even warrant a penalty of death (Exodus 21:15,17; Deuteronomy 21:18-21; 27:16). Honoring parents was one of the ten most important values God gave His chosen people (Exodus 20:12). Ham's unwillingness to cover his father's shame, choosing instead to gaze at him, perhaps led him to ridicule or scoff at Noah before his brothers. Ham's siblings, however, showed respect for their dad, covering up their father and being careful not to look on his naked body (Genesis 9:23).

50. 1 Kings 9:20-21.

Chapter 4—Carpenter Prophet

1. According to Luke 21:37, these private discourses may have actually taken place over the course of two days during Passion Week (Tuesday-Wednesday).

2. 2 Corinthians 5:21.

3. 1 John 2:2.

4. Found in Matthew 24:1–25:46, this is known as the Olivet Discourse and contains some of the most fascinating and significant prophetic material in the entire Bible.

5. Jesus' prediction literally came true 40 years later, in AD 70, when the Roman general Titus laid siege to Jerusalem. And exactly according Christ's words, he reduced the temple to rubble.

6. Luke 19:11.

7. Matthew 24:8.

8. Daniel 7:25; 9:27; 12:1,7; Matthew 24:21; Revelation 11:3; 12:6; 13:5. Some interpretative traditions see these prophecies as symbolic and not actual, while others interpret these apocalyptic events as having already occurred in the first century. See following endnote.

9. 1 Thessalonians 1:10; 4:13-18; 5:8-9. This word *rapture* doesn't appear in Scripture (but neither do the words *Trinity, Christianity, missionary,* or *Bible*). The word is an eschatological term used to describe the event mentioned in 1 Thessalonians 4:17. The Greek word Paul uses is from the verb *harpazo*, meaning, "to snatch away." Our word *rapture* comes from the Latin word *rapturo*, used when the original Greek word was translated into that language. It's simply a word that helps describe a biblical truth, like *Trinity.*

   The context of this section of Scripture (1 Thessalonians 4:13–5:11) is the end times and the deliverance of believers from God's wrath during "the day of the Lord" (1 Thessalonians 5:2; 2 Thessalonians 2:2; 2 Peter 3:10). However, some Christians, theologians, and denominations do not believe in a specific rapture event, but rather see a more symbolic interpretation of Revelation and the last days. The five main views of the rapture are:

   1. It happened already in the first century, in AD 70, but was spiritual, not literal in nature.
   2. It's purely symbolic, not actual.
   3. It's basically the same event as the second coming (post-Tribulation rapture).
   4. It occurs halfway through the Tribulation (mid-Tribulation rapture).
   5. It occurs just prior to the beginning of the Tribulation (pre-Tribulation rapture).

   This last view (#5) is the only one that sees Christ's return for His bride as imminent (or that it could occur at any time without warning). The other views make it fairly predictable.

10. Matthew 24:24.

11. 1 John 2:18.

12. 1 John 4:1-3.

13. See http://earthquake.usgs.gov/earthquakes/eqarchives/year/eqstats.php.

14. Off the coast of Italy, there lies the Marsili Volcano, the largest underground volcano in Europe. Nicknamed the Monster, volcanologists say its walls are fragile, making it "restless" and susceptible to imminent eruption. An eruption here would create a tsunami threatening all of southern Italy. Will this giant, and hundreds like it, be awoken during the Tribulation and utilized as a part of God's judgment on earth?

15. Revelation 6:3-6.

16. See Matthew 24:8.

17. John 6:37; Romans 10:13.

18. When Rome burned in AD 64, Nero blamed Christians. The Jews were blamed for the Black Plague. Satan doesn't need much reason to persecute those whom God loves, and during his final days on earth, any excuse will do.

19. Revelation 16:10-11.

20. See http://www.christianitytoday.com/article/number.of.christian.martyrs.continues.to.cause .debate/34673.htm.

21. See Acts 7:55; Revelation 6:9-11.

22. See Revelation 20:4. Today, Muslim extremists publicly execute Christians, Jews, and other "infidels" in this way, choosing either to remove the head with a swift swing of the sword, or to slowly and barbarically saw the head off with a knife. These murders and martyrdoms, often videotaped and circulated online, are but a preview of the horrific kind of death post-rapture believers will suffer at the hands of their persecutors.

23. See John 7:7; 15:18-21; Romans 12:18.

24. Mark 4:1-20; Luke 14:25-35.

25. Matthew 10:17-23; Matthew 24:13; 1 Peter 1:5. However, Jesus says the one who endures through this persecution demonstrates the genuineness of their faith.

26. 2 Timothy 2:11-12; Hebrews 3:12. The teaching of these false prophets could incite even more hatred toward those who profess faith in Jesus during the Tribulation.

27. Revelation 9:20-21.

28. See www.joshuaproject.net/great-commission-statistics.php.

29. Revelation 11:3-6.

30. There is debate among reputable Bible and prophecy experts whether the ministry of these two witnesses (Zechariah 4:12-13) will occur during the first or second 3½ years of the Tribulation. I understand Revelation 11:3-7 to indicate they will both be killed by the Antichrist after 1260 days of ministry. Such a public act would fit well with the "abomination of desolation" at the midpoint of the 7-year Tribulation, when he breaks his covenant with the Jews (Matthew 24:15; Daniel 9:27), desecrates the rebuilt Jewish temple in Jerusalem, and demands that the world worship him. Thus I see the two witnesses' ministry will be inaugurated at the *beginning* of the Tribulation.

31. Revelation 11:7-10. If the map of Israel in that day remotely resembles the map today (currently surrounded geographically by Arab countries), the death of the two Jewish witnesses preaching about a Jewish Messiah will be widely celebrated by Muslims, both locally and around the world (as well as by others).

32. Revelation 11:11-13.

33. Romans 11:25-26.

34. See Exodus 7:10; 8:1–12:29; 1 Kings 17:1; 18:41-45; 2 Kings 1:10-12.

35. Revelation 7:3-8.

36. Revelation 7:3. This identifying mark is also perhaps in contrast to the coming mark of the beast, seen in Revelation 13:16-18, which will similarly identify Antichrist's own followers.

37. Revelation 14:3-5.

38. These also likely contribute to the fulfillment of Romans 11:25-26.

39. Matthew 24:14; Revelation 14:6-7.

40. Revelation 14:6-7. We are told this angel will fly "in midheaven," quite possibly circling the earth as he simultaneously announces God's final offer of salvation.

41. This common question typically attempts to cast suspicion on the fairness of God in condemning those who die without Christ. There will be no excuse for those who live during the Tribulation, as everyone will hear the good news and be given opportunity to repent. But there is equal accountability for those who have lived prior to this as well. God has established an inner conscience in every person telling them there is a God, as well as displayed His attributes in the heavens and creation (Romans 1:18-23; 2:14-16). Rejecting the gospel is not God's only basis of condemnation. Simply being a sinner qualifies us for judgment. Even so, any person desiring to know this God will not be denied knowledge of Him, and anyone calling on Him for salvation will not be turned away (Isaiah 55:6-7; John 6:37; Romans 10:13-17; 2 Peter 3:9). When the end-times angel speaks, there will also be no confusion as to who this God is. See Psalm 2:8-10; Philippians 2:9-11.

42. Revelation 14:7.

43. 2 Peter 3:3-7.

44. The Bible has proven itself correct on issues related to history and science. Science is a great tool that has helped mankind in many areas. And yet it has also failed us as well. It has not successfully or sufficiently explained the origin or meaning of life, cured many diseases (including cancer), or prolonged life indefinitely. Science cannot speak with authority outside its areas of expertise. It is a field of study with inherent limits and boundaries. The Bible, however, though not a science book, has proven itself 100 percent accurate every time it speaks to matters of science, even predating many modern scientific discoveries. For example:

    - The roundness of the earth and cosmology (Isaiah 40:22).
    - The almost infinite extent of the universe (Isaiah 55:9).
    - The Law of Conservation of Mass and Energy (2 Peter 3:7).
    - The hydrologic cycle (Psalm 135:7; Ecclesiastes 1:7).
    - The vast, immeasurable number of stars (Jeremiah 33:22).
    - The law of increasing entropy, Second Law of Thermodynamics (Psalm 102:25-27).
    - The importance of blood in life processes, circulation of the blood (Leviticus 17:11).
    - Atmospheric circulation (Ecclesiastes 1:6).
    - The gravitational field, or that the earth hangs suspended in space (Job 26:7).
    - The mysterious force in the atom's substructure (Colossians 1:17).

    Clearly, God is a brilliant scientist!

45. 2 Peter 3:5-7,10-13.

46. Isaiah 45:5; 46:9-10; John 8:58; 10:30; Hebrews 1:2-3.

47. Revelation 16:9,11,21.

48. Luke 16:19-31. Today, those who seek evidence for God through miraculous signs and wonders will be disappointed. This is not to say God doesn't perform miracles in our day. But sending supernatural signs is not His primary way of convincing someone of His existence or the afterlife, according to Jesus. Even someone rising from the dead won't melt the coldness of the human heart and convince the mind. The real evidence, Jesus says, is found in the Word of God itself (Luke 16:30-31).

49. Daniel 9:27; Luke 21:20-24; 2 Thessalonians 2:4; Revelation 13:7-8,14-15.

50. Luke 21:20-22.

51. Matthew 24:3.

52. Matthew 24:32-34.

53. Matthew 24:33.

54. Matthew 24:36. While on the earth, Jesus chose to place complete trust in the Father for everything (John 8:28; 12:49-50; 14:31). He voluntarily gave up (laid aside) certain privileges and powers of deity, such as omnipresence, glory, and being worshipped by angels (Philippians 2:5-8; 2 Corinthians 8:9; Hebrews 2:9; Isaiah 6:3; Revelation 4:8-11; 5:6-14). He lived as a servant, revealing to His disciples only what the Father revealed to Him (John 15:15), voluntarily restricting His knowledge during His earthly ministry. Now glorified in heaven, He knows all things, including the exact timing of His return.

Chapter 5—A Godless World

1. 1 Corinthians 13:12-13.

2. Psalm 139:7-12. While God's omnipresence dictates that there is no place where His Spirit doesn't dwell, God does not manifest or reveal Himself every place He is.

3. Romans 1:19.

4. Psalm 19:1.

5. C.H. Spurgeon, *The Treasury of David*, vol. 1 (Peabody, MA: Hendrickson, n.d.), 271.

6. Psalm 10:4; 14:1; 53:1.

7. This denial and dismissal of God as Creator is obvious from Genesis 6:5,11-12. See also Psalm 14:1-3 and Romans 3:10-12.

8. Romans 1:22. The Greek word translated "fool" comes from a root word (*moros*) that those in the psychiatric community later adapted, coining the word *moron* around the turn of the twentieth century—see http://www.etymonline.com/index.php?term=moron.

9. Romans 1:24,26,28.

10. 2 Corinthians 12:21; Galatians 5:19; Ephesians 5:3; 1 Thessalonians 4:7.

11. Romans 1:24.

12. The issue of homosexuality is a controversial and heated one in our culture and world. Though Scripture is clear regarding the subject, the church has (particularly in recent decades) fumbled an awkward response to those who embrace this lifestyle. Beyond the obvious moral argument and the fact that choice is involved, there are other more complex contributing factors that lead some to become homosexual or some other sexual orientation. Physical, familial, relational, social, and emotional components also play a part. This complicated matter leads many to wrong, unbiblical conclusions.

God loves all homosexuals, and His desire is that they find their identity in Him and their salvation in Jesus. Homosexuality itself is not the sole issue keeping someone from going to heaven, but rather the sin principle within them. In the same way, merely quitting homosexuality (or adultery, thievery, etc.) doesn't automatically make someone righteous. Paul lists these particular sins as evidences of the greater sin problem within these persons. A pervasive lifestyle of sin (which Paul references in 1 Corinthians 6:9-11) is merely the outward fruit of the sin-filled heart. And though this particular sin-choice may directly contradict the natural created order of the male-female genders (unlike, for example, jealousy or anger), our root problem is *sin*, not *sins*. Paul's description in Romans 1 illustrates the truth that human sexuality relates to God's basic creation and the identity of humankind itself, thus the severity of His judgment against it. Finally, many Christians struggle with homosexual thoughts, feelings, and actions, just as they do with many other temptations—including various sexual sins.

13. That homosexuality is contrary to nature is a conclusion reached not requiring the existence of God. In other words, without introducing God into the argument, nature, biology, physiology, and logic argue against the justification for homosexuality.

14. Romans 1:28.

15. Romans 1:29-31. Every one of these self-fueled traits affects human relationships.

16. Romans 1:32.

17. 2 Thessalonians 2:10-12.

18. 1 Timothy 4:1; 2 Timothy 3:1; Hebrews 1:1-2; 1 John 2:18 even calls this age the "last hour."

19. Exodus 5:2,4.

20. Romans 9:17-18; Pharaoh hardened his heart ten times (Exodus 7:13,14,22; 8:15,19,32; 9:7,34,35; 13:15), and God hardened Pharaoh's heart ten times (Exodus 4:21; 7:3; 9:12; 10:1,20,27; 11:10; 14:4, 8,17). In seven of these instances, Pharaoh hardened his own heart before God hardened it.

21. Actually, Pharaoh's heart had long ago been layered with calloused unbelief. He followed almost word for word the pattern of Romans 1, from rejection of God's revelation in nature and conscience to Egyptian idolatry and ultimately believing himself to be a god. This brought total abandonment by God, along with eventual judgment.

22. Revelation 16:10-11,21.

23. Hebrews 10:26-31.

24. Hebrews 3:7-12.

25. Revelation 20:11-15.

26. Proverbs 26:11.

27. Isaiah 64:6.

28. Isaiah 53:6; 2 Corinthians 4:4; Ephesians 2:1.

29. 2 Thessalonians 2:3-9.

30. Another view sees this restrainer as representing government, since the Antichrist will have to make war and overcome kingdoms in his rise to prominence (Daniel 7:23-24; Revelation 6:2; 17:12-14).

31. Romans 8:9,11; John 14:17,23.

32. Hades was a Jewish euphemism for death—Job 38:17; Isaiah 38:10; Matthew 16:18.

33. John 11:25; Romans 6:9; 1 Corinthians 15:54-57; Hebrews 2:14; Revelation 1:18.

34. Throughout history, the persecution of believers has only advanced the cause of Christ.

35. Matthew 5:13-14.

36. See http://carm.org/religion-cause-war.

37. See http://www.probe.org/site/c.fdKEIMNsEoG/b.4220739/k.E4FC/The_Social_and_Hist orical_Impact_of_Christianity.htm, see also http://www.faithfacts.org/christ-and-the-culture/ the-impact-of-christianity.

38. Many non-Christian organizations provide positive services to humanity, particularly in helping the needy, improving quality of life, and promoting peace.

39. John 16:7-11. See also 2 Corinthians 5:16-17, where God changed Paul's perception of Christ, making him a new creation in Jesus. Satan's judgment was sealed at the cross (John 12:31), so is the judgment of unbelievers apart from salvation (John 3:36).

40. 1 John 4:4.

41. 2 Corinthians 4:4.

42. See also 2 Corinthians 4:4.

43. John 15:18-27.

44. 1 Corinthians 7:14. Paul described a believing wife as having a residual positive spiritual influence on her husband and children, making them "sanctified" or "holy." Similarly, individual Christians and authentic churches bring a sanctifying influence to their friends and communities, as well as an ambience of grace and decency. When those with godly values are removed, moral expediency and lawlessness will reign. Mysteriously, the Holy Spirit's presence in the world and in us is what holds back God's judgment, as in the case of Methuselah, Noah, and Lot. When the Spirit (and believers) are removed, nothing will restrain sin or avert God's wrath.

Chapter 6—A History of Violence

1. See http://www.theguardian.com/world/2011/jul/22/iran-public-execution-human-rights?guni =Article:in%20body%20link.

2. Steven Pinker, *The Better Angels of Our Nature: Why Violence Has Declined* (New York: Penguin, 2012). This Harvard psychology professor argues in his 800-page book that we are a much better race than those who came before us. He attributes this evolution in goodness to, among other things, trade between countries, women's rights, literacy, and scientific reason.

3. Will and Ariel Durant, *The Lessons of History* (New York: Simon & Schuster, 2010), p. 81.

4. See http://www.cnn.com/2013/01/05/world/americas/mexico-juarez-killings-drop. Between 2007 and 2011 more than 9000 people were killed, with the peak coming in 2010, when Juarez saw a record 3116 homicides, or about 8 murders per day, according to figures released by the Chihuahua State Attorney General's office.

5. Many in the pre-Civil War American church tolerated this practice, as slavery was commonplace. In this sense, the church was simply a product of the age, reflecting its cultural values. And though first-century Christians were born into a culture where slavery existed, these believers were commanded and expected to treat slaves as brothers and equals. See Galatians 3:28; Philemon 15-16.

6. See Psalm 139:13-16. God is intricately involved in the development and formation of children in the womb. To intentionally interrupt this divine work of creation by taking life usurps His right and role in humanity.

7. Less than 1 percent of abortions are due to rape or incest—see http://www.operationrescue.org/ about-abortion/abortions-in-america.

8. Deuteronomy 22:13-29.

9. Leviticus 18:6; 20:11-14.

10. This estimated number of murders took place in just three months' time—see http://survivors-fund.org.uk/resources/rwandan-history/statistics.

11. See Proverbs 6:17; 31:8-10.

12. See http://www.guttmacher.org/pubs/fb_IAW.html.

13. To date, China aborts 13 million babies every year, or about 35,000 per day. Most are forced abortions. Data from China's National Family Planning Commission, as reported by *China Daily* and cited in: Vicky Jiang, "Of the 13 Million Abortions in China, Most Are Forced," *Epoch Times*, December 9, 2012, http://www.theepochtimes.com/n2/china-news/one-child-policy-abortions-in-china-most-are-forced-21819-all.html.

14. Even in the most extreme scenarios (pregnancy resulting from rape or incest), does it become morally right to punish the child, or to punish the rapist?

15. Revelation 6:10 affirms the righteous principle of avenging the death of those who are murdered. This principle was inaugurated by God Himself in Genesis 9:6.

16. Isaiah 5:20; see also Proverbs 17:15.

17. Judges 21:25.

18. Matthew 5:21-22.

19. See http://www.fbi.gov/about-us/cjis/ucr/crime-in-the-u.s/2011/crime-in-the-u.s.-2011/violent-crime/violent-crime; http://www.unodc.org/unodc/en/data-and-analysis/homicide.html.

20. Psalm 51:6; 1 Samuel 16:7.

21. See Genesis 4:8.

22. Jeremiah 17:9 (NKJV).

23. Matthew 23:27-28.

24. John 14:10,31.

25. See 2 Timothy 3:5.

26. See Ephesians 4:30-31.

27. Mark 7:20-23.

28. God desires for His children to pursue peace with all men if possible, and never to pay back evil for evil (Romans 12:14-21). Escalation is natural. Diffusion is not. We need His Holy Spirit to empower us toward peace, whether it's familial, racial, or relationship reconciliation.

29. 1 John 3:15.

30. Some ask, "But didn't God condone and even command violent acts in the Old Testament, even upon children?"

    Yes. There's no denying that God instructed Israel to kill the occupants of the land He had promised to them. His covenant nation was to be separate and holy, free from the evil influences of surrounding pagan nations. God deemed killing to be practically and morally justified for that era in history. The historical context also justified it, as Israel lived in a culture of terrorists and a "kill or be killed" world, generally speaking. God also commanded just retaliatory vengeance as well (1 Samuel 15:3; Psalm 135:8; 136:10; 137:9).

    The Flood was a very violent act as well. God destroyed a world that had become violent and corrupt. However, the New Testament (New Covenant or Agreement) inaugurated a new perspective, as Jesus challenged us to focus on changing hearts, not killing enemies. He shows a deeper side to the spirit of God's moral law (Ten Commandments) in His Sermon on the Mount.

However, neither Jesus, nor the rest of the New Testament, denies or hides Israel's legacy of violent conquest and warfare. On the contrary, some of these acts and individuals are honored and praised for "conquering kingdoms" and being "mighty in war" (Hebrews 11:33-34). Jesus' own disciples expected Him to lead them in revolt against oppressive Rome and establish His kingdom by force. Clearly, a preoccupation with pacifism wasn't prevalent either in the first-century culture or the early church. Paul recognized the God-ordained right of government to "bear the sword" (capital punishment) and bring "wrath on the one who practices evil" in order to maintain civil order and protect law-abiding citizens (Romans 13:4).

The following thoughts may help clarify this issue:

First, our human understanding struggles to reconcile a God who is both just and gracious. It's the same principle of Job 2:10, reconciling both blessing and "evil" coming from God. Exodus 34:6 speaks of the Lord's compassion and grace and forgiveness while the very next verse states not one guilty person will go unpunished. See also Romans 11:22.

Second, some have used the Bible to justify personal (or national) unwarranted violence. These people do not understand the Bible.

Third, Jesus was no stranger to violence and physical force. He chased out the moneychangers from the temple *by force* with a whip (John 2:15). He was also the victim of brutality, physical abuse, and cruelty. Crucifixion was a violent experience for Christ, and the Father blasted His violent wrath upon His Son.

Fourth, Jesus' return to earth will be intensely violent, as He will brutally slay His enemies (Revelation 19:11-16).

Fifth, in a world enveloped by sin and sinful people, violence is inevitable. And it will grow worse.

Sixth, violence is justified in some cases, such as:

- Direct acts of God (as demonstrated in Revelation)
- Israel (in the Old Testament)
- Present just causes for military conflict
- In defense of self or family
- Government punishment of murderers

Seventh, God (because He is God) possesses the prerogative to take any life He chooses or command that life be taken according to His righteous desire (as in the Old Testament). God's displeasure goes beyond the issue of violence itself, to the unsanctioned taking of human life. His anger with pre-Flood culture grew out of people taking one another's lives by force, and this rampant violence grieved the heart of God.

31. According to Revelation 6:4, during the Tribulation, violent slaughter will be widespread and universal.

Chapter 7—50 Shades of Immorality

1. Genesis 6:11-13.

2. Francis Brown, Edward Robinson, S.R. Driver, Charles A. Briggs, *A Hebrew and English Lexicon of the Old Testament* (Oxford: Brown, Clarendon Press, n.d.), s.v. *Shachath*. This word is used some 136 times in the Old Testament, and the various usages and root meaning of the word can be found on pages 1007-1008.

3. Exodus 32:7.

4. Exodus 32:6—"The people sat down to eat and to drink, and rose up to *play.*" Both the

immediate context and other usage of this particular word strongly suggest illicit sexual activity (cf. Genesis 26:8). Paul references this event in 1 Corinthians 10:7.

5. Before crossing the Jordan River, God's people became sexually intoxicated with Moabite women and their pagan gods. For this, God sent a plague, killing 23,000 Israelites (Numbers 25:1-9). In 1 Corinthians 10:8, Paul cites two separate incidents of Israel's immorality to illustrate God's anger toward this sin. For their sexual idolatry at Sinai, Moses ordered the sons of Levi to cleanse Israel from those primarily responsible, and 3000 were killed (Exodus 32:25-28).

6. Genesis 6:5.

7. Deuteronomy 32:10-11; Isaiah 43:4; Zechariah 2:8; John 3:16; Romans 5:8.

8. Genesis 3:1 (NIV).

9. Genesis 3:4-5.

10. Genesis 3:7-8.

11. Genesis 3:10.

12. Though forgiven and restored, their family was rocked with tragedy through sibling murder. It wouldn't be until their third son was born that they began seeing positive spiritual fruit again. The aftereffects of sin lingered on as humanity dealt with the sin curses pronounced on them (Genesis 3:14-20).

13. Genesis 3:15.

14. Genesis 2:22-25.

15. Genesis 18:20.

16. Genesis 13:13.

17. Jude 7.

18. Romans 1:26-27. Paul uses two specific Greek words to describe homosexuals (1 Corinthians 6:9; 1 Timothy 1:10). One refers to practicing homosexuals, while the other to an effeminate, passive person who allows himself to be taken advantage of sexually, as in the case of male temple prostitutes.

19. The word here is the same Hebrew word *yada*, used to describe sex between a man and woman (Genesis 4:1; 38:26; Judges 19). Here, it's an obvious reference to male-to-male sex.

20. Genesis 19:9.

21. Genesis 19:11.

22. Genesis 19:23-26. Charles Ryrie writes, "Deposits of sulphur (brimstone) and asphalt (Genesis 14:10) have been found in this area" (*The Ryrie Study Bible* [Chicago: Moody Press, 1978], p. 35). Near the southern tip of the Dead Sea, large amounts of sulfur deposits have been found as well as remnants of an ancient civilization. See http://www.arkdiscovery.com/sodom_&_gomor rah.htm.

23. 2 Peter 2:6-7.

24. It's true that all sin breaks God's standard. But all sin is *not* the same because not all sinful behavior carries the same natural or divine consequences. You won't get fired for stealing a paper clip from work, but you will get terminated for embezzling company funds.

25. Some wishing to justify homosexuality do so by claiming God destroyed Sodom and Gomorrah because of "inhospitality." The problem with this laughable interpretation is that there is zero justification for it anywhere in the Bible, not even from the one verse torn out of context

to justify it (Genesis 19:9). Besides, no one would call being inhospitable an "exceedingly grave" sin, prompting God to annihilate those cities.

26. When defending homosexuality, it is sometimes pointed out that Jesus said nothing about it. But this is incorrect. When addressing the issue of divorce, Jesus specifically quotes Genesis 1:27; 2:24; 5:2, affirming not only God's creation of distinct genders, but also confirming the accepted Jewish standard of His day—that man was made for woman, and that those two were designed to be "one flesh." The argument from silence is insufficient anyway, as Christ also doesn't directly address other sexual sins, such as pedophilia or bestiality. He does address adultery between male and female, however.

27. Matthew 11:20-24; Luke 10:10-13. Had the miracles Jesus performed in Capernaum been done in Sodom, they would have been spared judgment. However, God didn't do this, choosing instead to destroy them. Jesus' point was to highlight the deeper offense of not believing in Him, and the resulting greater judgment on those who reject Him. Refusing faith in God's provision for sin forfeits all hope of salvation, forgiveness, and heaven and is the "unpardonable sin" (Matthew 12:31-32). The angels did supernaturally strike the multitude with blindness. Sadly, this prejudgment miracle wasn't enough to soften their lust-filled hearts. Because the Holy Spirit convinces individuals of their need for Christ, that is why this sin of unbelief is called "blasphemy against the Spirit."

28. Isaiah 3:9; Jeremiah 23:14; Lamentations 4:6; Ezekiel 16:44ff.

29. Luke 17:28-30.

30. The actions, attitudes, and hateful words of certain religious groups have tarnished the name of Jesus in our country. God does not hate homosexuals. Typical of Satan, the devil uses groups like these to divert from Christ's message of heart salvation. These groups season their hateful message with Bible verses, causing people to think they're actually Christians.

31. The New Testament word translated "lust" means "strong desire," and in this context, strong *sexual* desire.

32. Galatians 6:1-3.

33. Prime-time television, cable networks, and adult pay-per-view all portray sexual innuendo, sex acts, nudity, and both soft and hard-core porn. Japanese TV recently debuted a reality show entitled *Orgasm Wars* (http://www.huffingtonpost.com/2013/11/15/orgasm-wars-video-japan-gay-straight-man-orgasm_n_4282083.html).

34. Unless otherwise noted, all stats here are from http://www.covenanteyes.com/pornstats.

35. See http://www.thetawellnesscenter.com/pornography-addiction/how-to-break-porn-addiction.html.

36. Happily married men are 61 percent less likely to look at porn; 56 percent of divorce cases involved one party having an obsessive interest in pornographic websites.

37. US Department of Justice, Posthearing Memorandum of Points and Authorities, at 1 (ACLU v. Reno, 929 F. Supp. 824, 1996).

38. See www.wnd.com/2006/07/37244.

39. See http://www.huffingtonpost.com/2013/02/03/super-bowl-sex-trafficking_n_2607871.html. Some 10,000 prostitutes were brought into Miami for the 2010 Super Bowl. These large-scale events are but the tip of the iceberg when it comes to what is actually happening to young women around the world.

40. See http://www.fbi.gov/stats-services/publications/law-enforcement-bulletin/march_2011/human_sex_trafficking.

41. Genesis 3:6 describes the forbidden fruit as "good," a "delight to the eyes," and "desirable."

42. Hebrews 11:25 highlights the fact that sin is pleasurable. If it wasn't, who would want it or be attracted to it?

43. See http://drjudithreisman.org.

44. Proverbs 27:20. Like death and the grave, the eyes of man are never satisfied. Certainly this is true when it comes to lust.

45. *Porneia* is used 25 times in the Greek New Testament.

46. Ephesians 4:22 says the "old self" is continually being "corrupted."

47. Mark 7:18-23.

48. Preferably from parents who know God, know their child, and also understand *themselves*.

49. I recommend http://www.covenanteyes.com for Internet accountability.

50. James 4:7-8.

51. Psalm 37:4.

52. 2 Corinthians 10:5.

53. Psalm 119:11; Philippians 4:8.

54. Matthew 5:27-28.

55. 1 Thessalonians 4:5.

56. That's the essence of 1 Thessalonians 4:6.

57. 1 Thessalonians 4:7.

58. 2 Timothy 3:1-4.

59. See http://www.brandeis.edu/projects/fse/judaism/docs/essays/same-sex-marriage.pdf.

60. Meaning men, not just women, were being given in marriage.

61. Revelation 9:21. Here, universal immorality (Greek, *porneia*) is listed among the most prevalent sins mankind refuses to turn from in the end times.

62. Isaiah 3:9 (NIV).

Chapter 8—Difficult Days

1. Benjamin Peirce, *A History of Harvard University* (Cambridge, MA: Brown, Shattuck, and Co., 1833), Appendix, p. 5, 1636 rules.

2. From *The Rebirth of America*, published by the Arthur S. DeMoss Foundation.

3. See Genesis 4:25.

4. Genesis 4:17-24. Scripture makes it clear that Cain's line took a different path from the beginning.

5. See Hebrews 6:19.

6. 2 Thessalonians 2:3-4. The word "apostasy" signifies a departure or leaving of the faith, presuming there was at one time an embracing of faith.

7. Because the Antichrist will appear to support the Jewish faith, and in light of his desecration of the temple, this is why Paul refers to this event as the "apostasy."

8. Daniel 9:27; 11:31; Matthew 24:15. This prophecy contains both a near and far fulfillment, referring originally to the time when Antiochus Epiphanes invaded Jerusalem in 186 BC, entering the temple and turning the altar into a shrine to Zeus, afterward sacrificing pigs on it.

9. 2 Thessalonians 2:4.

10. Revelation 13:11-15.

11. See Matthew 24:15-20.

12. 1 Timothy 4:1.

13. Jude 1:3 (NKJV).

14. Revelation 22:18-19.

15. 2 Thessalonians 2:2.

16. Romans 3:20; 8:3-8; Ephesians 2:8-9.

17. Colossians 2:20-23.

18. 1 Timothy 4:3.

19. 1 Timothy 4:2.

20. Acts 17:17-18,32.

21. 2 Corinthians 11:3.

22. 1 Corinthians 1:18-25.

23. John 3:18-20.

24. Matthew 19:9-11.

25. John 6:41-66.

26. In Matthew 22:37-39, Jesus says the second commandment is to "love your neighbor as your-self." The point Jesus was making was not to focus on self, but rather to focus on others. Yet we've turned it upside down, inverting its intended meaning. Given that Jesus understood how nat-urally selfish we are and how much care and affection we give ourselves, He was simply saying, "Show others the same treatment that you naturally show yourself."

27. See 1 Corinthians 6:20.

28. John 3:30.

29. See Philippians 4:10-13; 1 Timothy 6:8.

30. 1 Timothy 6:10,17-19.

31. 1 Corinthians 16:16; 1 Thessalonians 5:12-13; Hebrews 13:7,17,24; 1 Peter 5:1-3.

32. Matthew 24:12.

33. "Hold to a *form* of godliness"—the word translated "form" is the Greek word *morphosis*.

34. 2 Timothy 3:6-7.

35. See Matthew 7:21.

36. Matthew 7:22. Some of these miraculous deeds may be actual, and performed by demonic power.

37. Matthew 7:23; see also Revelation 20:15.

38. Matthew 25:31-46.

39. See http://www.christianitytoday.com/gleanings/2013/may/inside-look-at-church-attenders-who-tithe-most.html.

40. Ellen isn't her real name.

41. This is not to criticize the use of cutting-edge presentations, the pursuit of excellence, or to dis-parage service in ministries and programs. People are necessary in leading and serving. But are

we truly exercising spiritual gifts or simply working a volunteer job in the church? Are we serving activities or serving God? Is the tail wagging the dog?

42. 2 Timothy 4:3-4.

43. 1 Timothy 1:9-10.

44. 1 Timothy 6:3-5—much like the men in Acts 17:21.

45. 2 Timothy 3:12-13.

46. 2 Timothy 3:14-17.

Chapter 9—Coming with the Clouds

1. See http://www.titanicinquiry.org/USInq/USReport/AmInqRep04.php.

2. The rest of the message actually read, "Shut up. I am busy. I am working Cape Race." The *Titanic* maintained constant contact with Cape Race, Newfoundland, throughout its voyage.

3. 2 Peter 1:20-21.

4. See Acts 24:15; Romans 8:5; 15:4; Titus 2:13; Hebrews 6:19.

5. 2 Peter 3:3-4.

6. See 2 Peter 3:5-6.

7. Ephesians 4:18.

8. 2 Peter 3:5. The phrase "escapes their notice" is translated "they deliberately suppress this fact" by the New English Translation (*NET Bible*® copyright © 1996-2006 by Biblical Studies Press, L.L.).

9. Psalm 14:1; Proverbs 1:7,22; 13:16; 18:2; 29:9; Matthew 7:26; 1 Corinthians 1:27.

10. See Genesis 11:1-9.

11. Revelation 1:7; 22:7,12,20.

12. Hebrews 12:2; 1 Timothy 2:5; Hebrews 7:25; John 14:2.

13. Revelation 19:7-10; 1 Corinthians 3:10-15; 4:5; 2 Corinthians 5:9-10.

14. Revelation 16:16.

15. This valley was also the site of several Old Testament battles, including Barak's defeat of the Canaanites (Judges 4) and Gideon's battle with the Midianites (Judges 7).

16. For a more detailed description of these battles, see Mark Hitchcock, *The End* (Wheaton, IL: Tyndale House, 2012).

17. Zechariah 14:4.

18. See chapter 4.

19. See http://www.icr.org/article/5107/.

20. Revelation 19:13.

21. John 1:1-3; Colossians 1:15; Hebrews 1:3.

22. Zechariah 12:10; Revelation 1:7.

23. Revelation 19:11.

24. Compare this scenario and character of God in judgment to Genesis 18:25.

25. Revelation 19:12.

26. Revelation 19:16.

27. Zechariah 14:5; Matthew 25:31; 1 Thessalonians 3:13; 2 Thessalonians 1:7; Jude 14; Revelation 17:14; 19:11,14.

28. Revelation 19:11.

29. John 14:3; 1 Thessalonians 4:13-18.

30. Matthew 25:31; Acts 1:9-11.

31. Matthew 24:35.

32. Revelation 19:15.

33. Revelation 19:15.

34. Revelation 14:19-20.

35. Proverbs 11:21; Isaiah 13:11.

36. Romans 8:30.

37. See John 20:19; 1 Corinthians 15:42-49; Philippians 3:21.

38. Romans 8:29; 1 John 3:2.

39. Revelation 16:14.

40. Revelation 17:14.

41. John 3:19-20.

42. Revelation 19:17-18.

43. Revelation 19:9.

44. Revelation 19:17.

45. Revelation 16:4-7.

46. Revelation 14:7.

47. Hosea 8:7.

48. Revelation 16:19.

Chapter 10—The Open Door

1. Ecclesiastes 3:1.

2. In order for certain end-times events to occur, Israel must be established as a nation and return to its ancient home—Jeremiah 30:1-5; Ezekiel 34:11-24; 37; Zechariah 10:6-10.

3. Mark Hitchcock, *The End* (Wheaton, IL: Tyndale House, 2012), pp. 111-12.

4. 1 Thessalonians 4:16. Scripture doesn't say what Christ shouts. It could be something like "Come forth!" No one knows. But what we do know is that every true believer will recognize His voice (John 10:27-28; see also John 5:28; 11:43).

5. Revelation 8–11.

6. 1 Thessalonians 4:15-17.

7. 1 Corinthians 15:51-54.

8. 1 Corinthians 15:52.

9. Philippians 3:20; 1 Thessalonians 1:10; James 5:7-9; Jude 21; Revelation 3:11; 22:7,12,20.

10. Titus 2:13.

11. Hebrews 9:28.

12. 2 Corinthians 11:2; 1 John 3:3.

13. 1 John 2:28.

14. 1 John 2:29–3:1.

15. Matthew 25:14-30.

16. Matthew 25:13.

17. Genesis 6:22–7:1.

18. See 2 Corinthians 2:15-16.

19. John 15:18-21.

20. John 6:44; 1 Corinthians 2:14.

21. 1 Corinthians 6:9-11.

22. Isaiah 45:22 (kjv).

23. C.H. Spurgeon, Susannah Spurgeon, Joseph Harrald, *The Autobiography of Charles H. Spurgeon: 1834-1854*, vol. 1 (London: Passmore & Alabaster, 1897), p. 106.

24. Romans 10:13.

25. See Romans 10:14-15.

26. See Luke 12:48.

27. See 2 Corinthians 6:2.

28. See John 3:16,36; 16:7-11.

29. See John 10:10.

To learn more about Harvest House books and
to read sample chapters, visit our website:

www.harvesthousepublishers.com

HARVEST HOUSE PUBLISHERS
EUGENE, OREGON